BIG
MATH ACTIVITIES
FOR YOUNG CHILDREN

BIG
MATH ACTIVITIES
FOR YOUNG CHILDREN

for
Preschool, Kindergarten and Primary Children

James L. Overholt, Ed.D.
California State University
Chico, California

Jackie White-Holtz, M.Ed.
Pine Grove School
Pine Grove, California

Sydney S. Dickson, Ed.D.
California State University (emerita)
Chico, California

Delmar Publishers

an International Thomson Publishing company I(T)P®

Albany • Bonn • Boston • Cincinnati • Detroit • London • Madrid
Melbourne • Mexico City • New York • Pacific Grove • Paris • San Francisco
Singapore • Tokyo • Toronto • Washington

NOTICE TO THE READER

Publisher does not warrant or guarantee any of the products described herein or perform any independent analysis in connection with any of the product information contained herein. Publisher does not assume, and expressly disclaims, any obligation to obtain and include information other than that provided to it by the manufacturer.

The reader is expressly warned to consider and adopt all safety precautions that might be indicated by the activities herein and to avoid all potential hazards. By following the instructions contained herein, the reader willingly assumes all risks in connection with such instructions.

The publisher makes no representation or warranties of any kind, including but not limited to, the warranties of fitness for particular purpose or merchantability, nor are any such representations implied with respect to the material set forth herein, and the publisher takes no responsibility with respect to such material. The publisher shall not be liable for any special, consequential, or exemplary damages resulting, in whole or part, from the readers' use of, or reliance upon, this material.

Cover Design: Jay Purcell

Delmar Staff:
Publisher: William Brottmiller
Acquisitions Editor: Erin O'Connor Traylor
Production Coordinator: James Zayicek
Art and Design Coordinator: Jay Purcell

COPYRIGHT © 1999
By Delmar Publishers

an International Thomson Publishing company

The ITP logo is a trademark under license

Printed in the United States of America

For more information contact:

Delmar Publishers
3 Columbia Circle, Box 15015
Albany, New York 12212-5015

International Thomson Publishing Europe
Berkshire House
168-173 High Holborn
London, WC1V7AA
United Kingdom

Nelson ITP, Australia
102 Dodds Street
South Melbourne
Victoria, 3205 Australia

Nelson Canada
1120 Birchmont Road
Scarborough, Ontario
M1K 5G4
Canada

International Thomson Editores
Seneca 53
Colonia Polanco
11560 Mexico D. F. Mexico

International Thomson Publishing GmbH
Königswinterer Strasße 418
53227 Bonn
Germany

International Thomson Publishing Asia
60 Albert Street
#15-01 Albert Complex
Singapore 189969

International Thomson Publishing Japan
Hirakawacho Kyowa Building, 3F
2-2-1 Hirakawacho
Chiyoda-ku, Tokyo 102, Japan

ITE Spain/ Paraninfo
Calle Magallanes, 25
28015-Madrid, Espana

1 2 3 4 5 6 7 8 9 10 XXX 04 03 02 01 00 99 98

Library of Congress Cataloging-in-Publication Data

Overholt, James L.
    Big math activities for young children / by James L. Overholt,
Jackie White-Holtz, Sydney S. Dickson.
        p.   cm.
    Includes bibliographical references and index.
    ISBN 0-7668-0018-0
    1. Mathematics—Study and teaching (Preschool–Kindergarten–Primary)—
Activity programs.   I. White-Holtz, Jackie.   II. Dickson, Sydney S.   III. Title.
QA135.5.09   1998
372.7—dc21   98-3263
                                                               CIP

Contents

About This Resource

What mathematical experiences are important for children? Teachers and parents are concerned that *their* children be provided with first-hand experiences that will allow them to understand and become proficient with mathematics. Teachers do their best to provide such activities, but between teaching classes, planning lessons, preparing materials, and numerous other responsibilities they just don't have additional hours to spend on developing appropriate tasks. Parents, on the other hand, are often uncertain about which mathematics activities are appropriate for young children. *Big Math Activities for Young Children* provides a wide selection of activities and investigations that will help each learner understand and/or practice the mathematics that he or she is expected to master.

Many of the suggested activities can be experienced as either in-class or at-home tasks. However, since parental involvement generally has a favorable effect on behavior and learning, it is recommended that a number of the activities be used as homework. According to research, meaningful and appropriate homework assignments have proven to be an effective method of increasing skills and understanding. Such mathematics homework must be well planned, presented in a positive manner, and needs to provide students with the opportunity to practice problem-solving skills. However, the process of the activity, rather than task completion, should be the goal. That is, the activities should be fun and engaging for both parent and child; it is better to have brief *play* sessions that are mutually satisfactory than to have longer ones that end in strife or hurt feelings. *Big Math Activities for Young Children* provides opportunities for many hands-on interactions that can help students with the conceptualization of often abstract ideas.

In summary, this book combines the helpful nature of meaningful and appropriate homework with the beneficial power of parental involvement. Teachers or parents can use the included activities to make a connection between math concepts in class and problem solving at home. The suggested tasks in *Big Math Activities for Young Children* focus on Number Sense and Counting, Number Operations, Measurement, Geometry, and Problem Solving and Reasoning. The activities are designed for use with kindergarten and first grade learners; however, the included More Advanced Variations note how to use them with older or more capable students, and the Easier Variations also provide for their use with preschoolers.

Finally, it should be noted that the authors bring a wealth of related experience to this book. One is a classroom teacher and a parent; another is an Early Childhood Education specialist, a former teacher, and a parent; and the third is a specialist in Mathematics Education, a former classroom teacher, and a parent. As such, they are quite sure that the provided activities will help to increase parent/child and teacher/child verbal interaction and develop a positive attitude toward math at an early age. The activities can also help to create closer relationships.

ABOUT THE AUTHORS

James L. Overholt, Ed.D. (University of Wyoming, Laramie) has been exploring the use of manipulative and visual materials available for mathematics instruction since the 1960s. As a parent, an elementary teacher, a university professor, and the author of five other "how to learn mathematics" books, his investigations have taken him into preschool through grade 12 classrooms and to adult mathematics learning workshops. He is currently Professor of Education at California State University, Chico.

Jackie M. White-Holtz, M.Ed. (California State University, Chico) teaches kindergarten at Pine Grove School in Pine Grove, California, and serves on the Amador County Curriculum Council. Previously she taught a first/second grade combination class, a fourth/fifth grade combination class, and a kindergarten through fourth grade multigraded class. Her Master's program focused extensively on appropriate mathematics activities for kindergarten/first grade children as well as stimulating parental involvement in this realm. Mrs. White-Holtz is married and the mother of a daughter.

Sydney S. Dickson, Ed.D. (University of Illinois, Champaign-Urbana) recently retired from the faculty of California State University, Chico, where she was a Professor of Education specializing in Early Childhood Education. In addition to being a parent, she worked with elementary student teachers for 17 years and taught courses in ECE curriculum development and children's literature. For the past ten years, she served as Coordinator of the Interdisciplinary Child Development Program. Prior to these activities, Dr. Dickson was a teacher in the Child Development Preschool Laboratory program at the University of Illinois. She has also taught kindergarten and first grade.

Suggestions for Using Big Math Activities

The selection of activities from this resource should be based on (1) the needs and interests of students, (2) prior experiences the child has had, and (3) how the tasks relate to classroom curriculum. The activities in each chapter have been placed in a usable order, but they do not need to be done sequentially; furthermore, the activities from various chapters can be used simultaneously. Thus, the teacher or parent should select activities that are interesting and understandable for the intended learner(s). To assist with this endeavor, the following format is provided for each activity:

WHY DO IT?

This section notes briefly where the activity fits into the curriculum and explains what the activity hopes to accomplish.

HERE'S HOW!

This segment provides information on materials needed and directions to complete the activity. (Most materials needed are readily available at home or in the classroom. Directions for constructing others are provided in Appendix A.)

VARIATIONS:

Variations are provided for each activity to accommodate a wide range of childrens' learning abilities. Although the tasks were designed initially for kindergarten and first grade children, the *Easier* and *Advanced Variations* also provide for their use with preschoolers as well as older or more capable students. The *Easier Variations* provide a more basic introduction to the concept or process, whereas the *Advanced Variations* provide a challenge and stimulate slightly different thinking skills.

■ APPENDIXES

Included are additional sources and resources including:

A. Simple Equipment to Make or Acquire (such as Milk Carton Dice and Paper Clip Spinners).

B. Selected Resources for Use with Young Children (an Annotated Book List and Computer Software).

C. Selected Sources for Parents and Teachers (Books, Magazines, Video Tapes and World Wide Web Internet Sites).

D. Recommended Developmental Experiences (Matching, Grouping, Patterning, Seriation, Beginning Number Concepts, All or Part Of, Measuring and Estimating and Problem Solving and Reasoning).

CHAPTER 1

Number Sense and Counting

Children must learn to deal with counting and number concepts from an early age. Young learners soon realize that they would rather have three cookies than one or that they would prefer to have more than one piece of candy. Children begin to develop number sense through such experiences. Their first counting attempts are generally accomplished in a rote fashion, but they soon realize that some numbers tell *how many* (cardinal numbers), whereas others designate *position or order* (ordinal numbers). With proper experiences, the learners will realize that a quantity is represented by a name and a written numeral (••• is named **three** and written as the numeral **3**). They begin with a vague sense of simple fractions and in time learn about the need for equal parts. They are shown how to manipulate ones and tens and in time discover place value concepts. The activities provided in this chapter help young children to deal effectively with a wide range of needed number sense and counting concepts.

1

Number Search Walk

■ WHY DO IT?

To develop number/numeral* recognition skills

To foster an awareness of numbers in the learner's surroundings

■ HERE'S HOW!

1. Go on a short walk in or around the classroom, the child's home, and/or the neighborhood.
2. While on the walk help the learner find as many numbers as possible. Examples include those on clocks, signs, calendars, houses, license plates, price tags, or telephones. Allow the learner to talk about the numbers and their importance.

---

*In a strict sense "number" refers to a quantity (there were four cookies in the jar), whereas "numeral" refers to the sign or symbol used to express the quantity (4 or four). However, since most people would call 4 a number, both number and/or numeral activities in this book will be termed "number activities."

3. Ask the learner to draw a picture of at least two places where he found numbers or have him dictate a list for you to write down of places where numbers were found.

AN ALTERNATE VARIATION:

1. Find pictures of numbers in magazines or newspapers.
2. Have the learner cut them out and help her to make a collage or scrapbook.
3. Discuss what the numbers mean and also how the same numbers appear in various settings, such as a $2 item versus Apt. #2 versus 2:00 on a digital clock.

AN EASIER VARIATION:

1. On index cards or small sheets of paper make two sets of cards numbered 0 through 9.
2. Have the learners match the numbers and put them together in sets.

AN ADVANCED VARIATION:

1. Numbers are often written in different forms, such as 4, **4**, 4, 4, 4, *4*, and **4**. Help the learner become familiar with several such number forms.
2. Have the learner use a calculator to match a number found in an everyday setting.
3. Cut out samples from newspapers or magazines and have the learner match figures that represent the same number.
4. Ask the learner to arrange the numbers in numerical order.

ANOTHER ADVANCED VARIATION:

1. A number game might be played at home, at school, in the grocery store, or when riding in the car by asking the learner to find numbers and to call them out.
2. The game might be played by first locating a "1," and then a "2," followed by a "3," and so forth. (Allow young learners to use numbers wherever they might find them. For example, it is just fine if he locates a "2" in the license plate number 527BVX such as in the illustration.)
3. Another time the game might be played by having the learner locate the number "5" as many times as possible.

Find That Number

■ WHY DO IT?

To recognize numbers

To practice finding *how many* each number is

■ HERE'S HOW!

1. Photocopy the *Find That Number Game Board* (see below), and provide *a dot die* (see Appendix A for directions on making or modifying dice) and a different marker for each player.
2. A player rolls the dot die and moves to the first space on the game board containing the corresponding number.
3. The next player rolls the dot die and moves her marker to a corresponding number box. Two players may occupy the same space.
4. The game continues until one player reaches the end. To complete the game, the player must roll the exact number shown in the end square.

■ AN EASIER VARIATION:

1. Make a set of puzzle cards and provide markers such as beans or pennies.
2. Draw a dividing line down the center of each card. Write a number on one half and draw the corresponding number of figures on the other.
3. Have the learner place a marker on each figure, count the markers, point to the number, and say the number name.

■ ADVANCED VARIATIONS:

1. Make a *Find That Number Game Board* with numbers from 7 to 12 and construct a **dot die** using amounts from **7 to 12.** As in the earlier game, the learner counts the number of dots rolled and moves to the corresponding number on the board.
2. Learners who need a further *challenge* might add the numbers together from the two 1 to 6 dice, to determine where they should place their markers.

FIND THAT NUMBER GAME BOARD

| START 5 | 1 | 12 | 3 | 8 | 11 | 2 | 6 | 5 | 12 | 4 | 10 |

9
3
1

| 5 | 4 | 6 | 9 | 1 | 11 | 3 | 10 |

2

| 11 | 12 | 6 | 1 |

| 8 | 5 | 2 | 12 |

7

10

| 7 | 3 | 2 | 5 | 1 | 8 | 12 | 4 |

7
2
1

| 3 | 2 | 5 | 9 | 10 | 1 | 4 |

11

12

6

| 7 | 4 | 8 | 11 | 3 | 9 |

9 | 2 | 10 | 5 |

1 | 4 | 7 | 12 | 1 |

THE END 5

| 5 | 12 | 8 | 3 | 11 | 6 | 4 | 10 | 2 |

Number Write

■ **WHY DO IT?**

To practice number (numeral)* formation

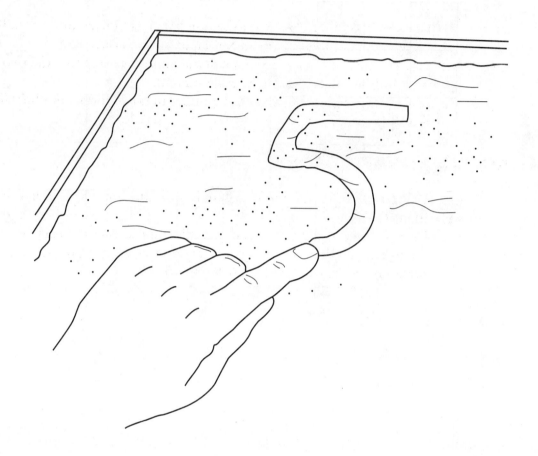

■ **HERE'S HOW!**

1. Give the learner a pan or small box with a thin layer of sand, salt, or corn meal spread evenly across the bottom. Have the learner use his finger to practice writing numbers in the sand or other medium. After successfully writing one number, shake the pan gently to erase that number and ask the learner to write a different number.

---

*In a strict sense "number" refers to a quantity (there were four cookies in the jar) while "numeral" refers to the sign or symbol used to express the quantity (4 or four). However, since most people would call "4" a number, both number and/or numeral activities in this book will be termed number activities.

2. To obtain a similar tactile experience use a small amount of shaving cream spread on a flat surface such as a cookie sheet or tabletop (or any surface that can be washed off easily). Have the learner use her finger to practice writing the numbers from 0 to 9. If a more permanent record of achievement is desired, use finger paint to create a number picture. (A recipe for homemade finger paint appears in Appendix A.)

AN EASIER VARIATION:

1. Construct tactile cards by gluing numbers cut from sandpaper, felt, or some other textured material to cardboard or large index cards.
2. Have the learner trace the shape of the numbers using the first two fingers (pointer and middle fingers) of his dominant hand.
3. Then have the learner write the number in the air or on another surface. Don't use a pencil and paper.

ADVANCED VARIATIONS:

1. Using a set of tactile number cards, have the learner close her eyes and feel and identify the numbers.
2. Use a variety of materials such as fabric, pipe cleaners, beans, or popcorn and have the learner construct her own set of tactile cards by gluing numbers made from the materials on index cards or poster board.

Number Bake

■ WHY DO IT?

To practice number/numeral* formation

To be exposed to the "how manyness" of numbers

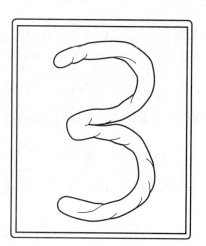

■ HERE'S HOW!

1. Fold five sheets of typing paper in half and write large numbers from 0 to 9 with one number on each half.
2. Make up your favorite cookie recipe adding about an extra 1/2 cup of flour to make the dough stiffer or use the recipe on the next page. Help the learner roll the dough into fairly thin snakes and shape them to match the drawn number patterns.
3. The learner might add raisins or M&M's in the appropriate quantity for each number (such as placing one raisin on the number 1, two raisins on the number 2).
4. Gently remove the dough numerals from the number patterns and place them on cookie sheets. Bake according to directions, talk about the finished numerals, and enjoy eating them!

---

*In a strict sense "number" refers to a quantity (there were four cookies in the jar) while "numeral" refers to the sign or symbol used to express the quantity (4 or four). However, since most people would call "4" a number, both number and/or numeral activities in this book will be termed number activities.

Attack Cookies

3 cups oatmeal   *1½ cups flour*

1½ cups butter   *1½ teaspoons baking powder*

Dump ingredients in a large bowl.

Mix it! Mush it! Knead it! Pound it! Attack it!

Shape as numbers and place on a cookie sheet.

Bake at 350 degrees for 10–12 minutes.

■ AN EASIER VARIATION:

1. Read the book *Count Worm*[1] with the learners.
2. Help the learners to use pipe cleaners or segments of pliable electric wire to make their own *Count Worm* numbers.
3. If the learners wish to make their worms look like those in *Count Worm,* paper hats and eyes may be glued to the pipe cleaners.

■ AN ADVANCED VARIATION:

1. Make a birthday plaque for a friend or family member by using hardening play dough (see Appendix A for directions) or clay and a piece of heavy cardboard or wood for backing.
2. Form the appropriate numbers for the birth date or age and glue them to the backing.
3. Decorate the plaque with paint, beads, glitter, or artificial flowers. A string or other hanger may be attached if desired.

Number Book

◾ WHY DO IT?

To increase number sense

To practice arranging numerals in order

◾ HERE'S HOW!

1. Have the learner draw, write, or glue a picture of one item and write a number 1 on the page.
2. Have the learner draw, write, or glue two pictures of the same type and write the number 2 on the next page.
3. Continue this process up to the number 10. Make a cover for the book entitled "————'s (the student's name) Number Book." Fasten the pages together in order. Have the learner share the book with someone else.

◾ EASIER VARIATIONS:

1. Use 3 × 5 index cards or paper. Write a number on one part of each card and draw the corresponding number of figures on the other. Cut the cards to make two-piece puzzles.
2. To play, the learner must match each number and quantity by putting the puzzle pieces together.

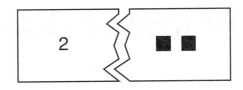

3. After putting all the puzzles together for numbers one through five (or for numbers one through ten) have the learner lay them in a line in numerical (sequential) order.

4. To provide a related tactile experience, make a set of cards where white glue is put on each figure and the outline of each number. Sprinkle salt, corn meal, or glitter on the damp glue and allow the mixture to dry before shaking off the excess. The learner should then gently trace the forms with her finger for a prewriting experience.

■ AN ADVANCED VARIATION:

1. Create a booklet of everyday number findings.
2. Have the learner print a 1 on top of the first page, a 2 on the second page, and so forth, for each number up to 10 or beyond.
3. On the appropriate pages have the learner paste pictures of, or make drawings of, or write a list of a number of everyday things that correspond. For example, on the 1s page might be a picture of a dog with 1 tail, a drawing of a flower with 1 stem, or a notation that I can wash my hands in 1 minute. The 2s page might include references to 2 hands, 2 feet, 2 eyes per person, or 2 wheels on a bicycle.
4. When the learner is ready, fasten the pages together in order and have him or her share the book with someone else. This is a great activity for parents and children to do together!

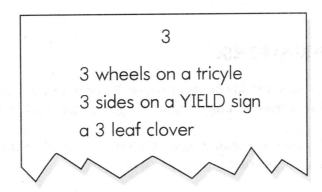

■ ANOTHER ADVANCED VARIATION:

1. Have the learner use dot paper (Appendix A) to create loop diagrams.
2. Begin, for example, with 10 dots and with a pencil or crayon loop as many groups of 2 as possible; also have the learner count the resulting diagram by 2s, such as 2, 4, 6, 8, 10.
3. Talk about how many 2s it took to make 10; it is hoped the learner will begin to understand that five 2s make 10, and, in time, 5 times 2 = 10 and conversely 10 divided into groups of 2 = 5 groupings.
4. If the learner understands the process, continue by having her determine how many 3s are in 10 (consider that there is a remainder of 1); also how many 4s, 5s, and so on.
5. When the learner appears ready, use 20 dots, 30 dots, 40 dots, and so on up to 100 dots. This activity serves as a basis for helping to understand multiplication and division.

Calendar Game

■ WHY DO IT?

To practice counting up to 6

To develop number recognition

To practice addition and subtraction

■ HERE'S HOW!

1. Get a page from an old calendar and a marker such as a bean or a small stone for each player and a die marked 1 through 6. (See Appendix A for instructions on how to make or modify dice).
2. Each player starts before the number 1 and takes a turn rolling the die to determine how many spaces he gets to move on the calendar page. Take time to count the number of spaces moved as well as to discuss the number landed on.
3. The first player to reach the final number on the calendar page wins.

■ AN EASIER VARIATION:

1. Get a page from an old calendar, a marker for each player, and a die marked 1 through 6.
2. A player rolls the die and moves to the first space on the calendar that has that number in it. (Place value is not taken into consideration in this game.) For example, if the first roll is a 4, the player moves to the 4. If his next roll is a 1, the player moves to the 10 because of the 1 in 10. By next rolling a 5, the player moves to the 15, and so forth.

■ ADVANCED VARIATIONS:

1. The learner plays the same game as in the original activity, however, she must calculate before moving which calendar square will be landed on. If the learner is capable, this might be accomplished by adding the current space occupied to the number rolled on the die.)
2. To practice subtraction, the players may start from the last number on the calendar and move toward the 1 space.

Leg Count

■ WHY DO IT?

To practice counting, categorizing, and keeping records

■ HERE'S HOW!

1. Have the learner look at furniture, people, and/or animals and tell how many legs each has.
2. Record on a chart such as this one how many legs each has.

Number of Legs: Item:	1	2	3	4	5	6 or more
DOG				X		

AN EASIER VARIATION:

1. Give the learner four small pieces of paper and ask that he try to find items that have four legs.
2. When the learner thinks he has found something with four legs, have the pieces of paper matched with each leg. This can be accomplished by lifting each leg and putting a paper directly under it or by just placing one paper by each leg.
3. Repeat to find something else with four legs. Continue by looking for items with 1 leg or 2 legs or 5 legs and so on.

AN ADVANCED VARIATION:

Have the learner list as many objects as possible that come in ones, twos, threes, fours, and so on up to ten. For example, noses come in 1s as do mouths, eyes come in 2s and so do ears. Tricycles have 3 wheels, and so forth.

ANOTHER ADVANCED VARIATION:

Locate and list products that are sold in select size groups and/or that have a number in the name. For examples 1-a-Day® multiple vitamins has a 1 in the name and is usually sold 1 container at a time, whereas 7Up® has a 7 in the name and is often sold in 6-packs.

Musical Count

◼ WHY DO IT?

To practice counting from one to ten

To better understand the "how manyness" of numbers

◼ HERE'S HOW!

1. To the tune of "Jingle Bells" sing the following:
   One, two, three
   Four, five, six
   Seven, eight, nine, ten
   All these numbers are my friends
   From one right up to ten.

Chords: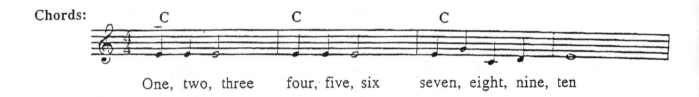

One, two, three   four, five, six   seven, eight, nine, ten

All these numbers   are my friends   from one right up to ten.

2. Use your fingers to show the numbers as you sing the song. Put up one finger while you sing "one," a second finger up while you sing "two," and so on.
3. Use some small objects such as pebbles, beans, or small candies to build a visual picture of each number in the song. For example, put one pebble on a card, put two pebbles on the next card, and three pebbles on the next card, and so on. Then sing the song while pointing to the corresponding cards.

■ AN EASIER VARIATION:

Use this song (or another song) as an echo. The adult sings one line and the learner echoes that line. Continue to the number ten and repeat several times.

■ ADVANCED VARIATIONS:

1. Make cards that have the numbers 1 through 10 printed clearly on them. Have the learner point to the written number while singing the above song.
2. Make up a similar counting song to the same melody or to another familiar tune. Songs such as "This Old Man" and "Over in the Meadow" might be used.

Hang That Number

■ **WHY DO IT?**

To practice arranging the numbers 1 through 10 in numerical order

■ **HERE'S HOW!**

1. Photocopy and cut out the cards numbered 1 through 10 and hang a string between two chairs.

1	2	3	4	5
6	7	8	9	10

2. Have the learner hang the numbers in order on the string and attach them with clothes pins. If you don't have clothes pins, fold over the top of each number card and hang it from the crease.

◼ AN EASIER VARIATION:

1. Before beginning the task of hanging the numbers, provide a number line for the learner to observe.
2. Have the learner match the order as he hangs the numbers 1 through 10.

$$0 \quad 1 \quad 2 \quad 3 \quad 4 \quad 5 \quad 6 \quad 7 \quad 8 \quad 9 \quad 10$$

◼ ADVANCED VARIATIONS:

After the numbers 1 through 10 are hung in order, have the learner close her eyes or turn around. Then try one or more of the following activities.

1. Switch two or more numbers around and ask the learner to rearrange them in the correct order.
2. Remove a number leaving a space. Ask the learner which number is missing. Then replace it.
3. Remove one or more numbers and squeeze the remaining numbers together. Ask the learner which numbers are missing. Then replace them.
4. Instead of providing the learner with numbers you have removed, provide blank cards so she can write the missing numbers and place them in the line.
5. Make cards numbered 11 through 20 and add them to the set. Repeat the procedures outlined above.

Table Math

■ WHY DO IT?

To practice rote and rational counting

To match numbers and items on a one-to-one basis

■ HERE'S HOW!

1. Ask the learner to count out enough plastic or metal knives, forks, and spoons to set the table for her family. Then have the learner check for accuracy by distributing them as if setting the table.
2. As an alternate in-school activity, have the learner count out and distribute enough napkins for each person at snack time.

■ AN EASIER VARIATION:

Provide a number of items or pictures of items and ask the learner to count them, pointing to each one as it is counted.

■ ADVANCED VARIATIONS:

1. Provide two sets of items or pictures of items that go together, such as forks and spoons, or pictures of dogs and dog houses. Ask the learner to count the individual items and then put them together in appropriate pairs.
2. As a *fun extension,* read the book *The Doorbell Rang*[2] by Pat Hutchins. Make a dozen cookies from brown paper grocery bags. Have the learners count, distribute, and redistribute the cookies as the story is read.

Eatable Math

WHY DO IT?

To practice counting accurately

To estimate numbers of items

HERE'S HOW!

1. Provide a bowl of raisins, popcorn, or cereal and set out cards numbered from 1 through 10 face up.
2. Have the learner place the appropriate number of items on each card. If the learner is correct, the items may be eaten, such as 4 Cheerios® from the 4 number card.
3. If the learner appears ready, make cards numbered from 11 through 20 and continue the activity.

EASIER VARIATIONS:

1. Place a number of raisins or cereal pieces on a plate. Ask the learner to count them and if he is correct, let him eat them.
2. Call out a number from 1 to 10 and ask the learner to count out the appropriate number of eatable items. If he is correct, the items may be eaten.

AN ADVANCED VARIATION:

1. Have the learner estimate (guess) how many raisins will fit into a teaspoon or a tablespoon?
2. Have the learner fill the spoon with the raisins and then count them.
3. The learner might also guess whether more raisins or cereal bits will fit in the spoon and then compare and count to find the difference.

ANOTHER ADVANCED VARIATION:

1. Give a slice of raisin bread to each learner.
2. Ask whether all the slices will have the same number of raisins in them?
3. Find out how many raisins each piece has.
4. Discuss whose slice has the most, and whose has the least. Predict how many raisins will be in the entire loaf.

Capture the Critter

■ WHY DO IT?

To practice counting to 10

To develop logical reasoning skills

■ HERE'S HOW!

1. Photocopy and cut out the critter, the game board strips, and the die numbered 0 through 5 below. Glue the strips together at the stars so that only one star shows at the center and 10 spaces extend in either direction to the ends. Also assemble the dice (or see Appendix A for directions on how to make or modify dice) and fold the critter so it will stand.
2. Place the critter on the star in the center of the game strip.
3. Have the players sit opposite each other and place the game strip with one end toward each player.
4. Player #1 rolls a die and moves the critter marker that many spaces toward herself.
5. Player #2 then rolls a die and moves the critter marker back toward himself.
6. The first player to move the critter to his or her end wins.

■ AN ALTERNATE VARIATION:

1. Use masking tape to designate 15 tile squares in a row (such as floor or countertop tiles) or draw 15 squares with chalk on a sidewalk and place an *X* on the middle square.
2. Place a favorite marker such as a teddy bear or even a person on the *X*.
3. Players stand opposite each other with the tile squares between them.
4. The first player rolls a die numbered 1 through 6 and moves the marker that many spaces toward herself.
5. The second player rolls the die and moves the marker back toward himself.
6. The first player to move the marker all the way to his or her end of the tiles wins.
7. If the players appear ready for greater *challenges,* variations might include increasing the length of the tile rows and/or playing with two dice. Additionally, teams of learners could work together to play this game.

■ AN ADVANCED VARIATION:

1. Photocopy the 13 × 13 grid and the critter to play an advanced variation of *Capture the Critter.*
2. Two to four players are required with each one sitting on a separate side of the grid. A single critter is placed on the star in the middle of the grid.
3. Each player takes a turn rolling one die (numbered 1 through 6) and moves the critter either vertically, horizontally, or diagonally.

CAPTURE THE CRITTER GAME PIECES

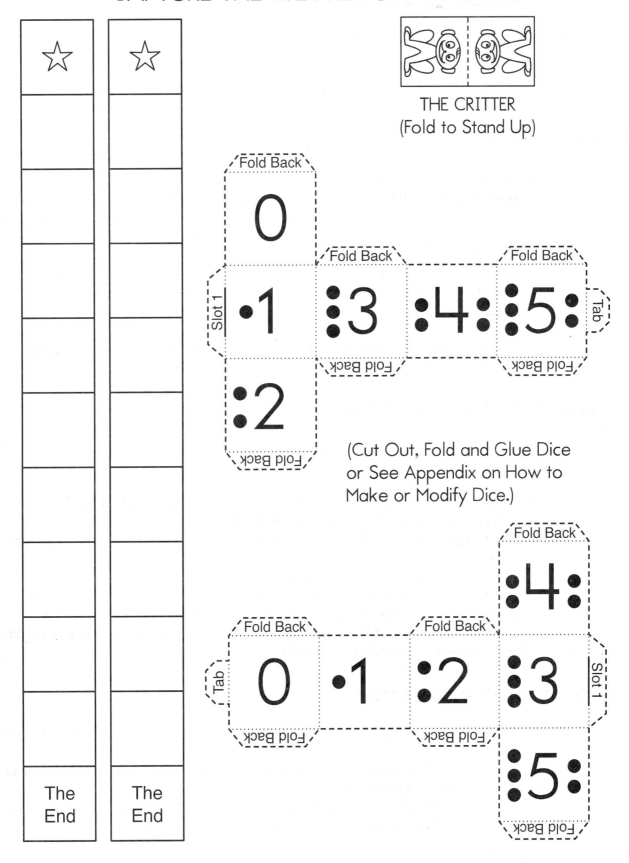

THE CRITTER
(Fold to Stand Up)

(Cut Out, Fold and Glue Dice
or See Appendix on How to
Make or Modify Dice.)

4. The object of the game is to be the first player to move the critter off his or her side of the grid.

5. More *challenging variations* may be achieved by using a grid that is 25 × 25 squares (photocopy and glue four of the 13 × 13 grids together) or larger and playing the game as described above, using two dice.

THE CRITTER

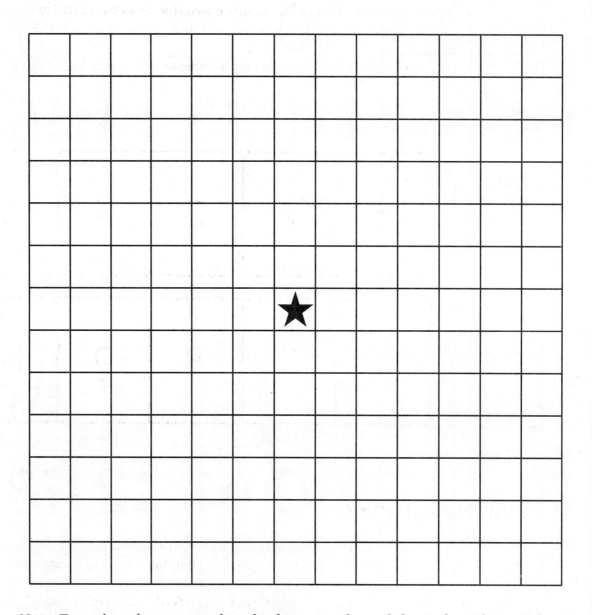

Note: To make a larger game board, photocopy four of the inch grid pages from Appendix A and glue or tape them together.

Before and After

■ WHY DO IT?

To reinforce number order

To learn before, after, one more, one less, and so forth

■ HERE'S HOW!

1. Photocopy and cut apart the number cards (or make your own) and mix their order.
2. Show the learner a card and ask which number comes after. Repeat for all the cards.
3. Try again, this time asking which number comes before.

1	2	3	4	5

6	7	8	9	10

■ EASIER VARIATIONS:

1. Write the numbers 1 through 5 in a row (a number line). Have the learner point to each number and identify it by name. Help the learner with the name if necessary. Later do numbers 6 through 10.
2. Teach the words "in front of" and "in back of," and "before" and "after." Then ask the learner to point or put a marker on the number in front of 2 or after 4. Practice various phrases as long as the learner is attentive.

3. A less difficult task might be to have the learner begin with the number 1 and place the cards in order. If assistance is needed, you might also print dots on the cards.

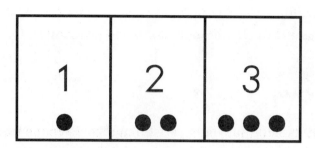

ADVANCED VARIATIONS:

1. Instead of using the word "after," use "one more." Instead of using the word "before," use "one less." Other words with similar meanings such as "greater" and "fewer" might also be used.

2. If the learners appear ready, try numbers that are two more or two less, and so forth. As a further *challenge,* have the learners consider which number is two less than two, two less than one, and so forth.

3. Try some counting on a calculator by pressing 1 + 1 and have the learners state the outcome before pressing the equals button. Continue by having the learners tell what might happen each time the equals button is pressed. (*Note:* Most calculators will read out 2, 3, 4, and so forth. Try your calculator in advance to make sure this works.) You might also try subtraction where, for example, $10 - 1 = 9 = 8 = 7$, and so forth.

Two by Two

▦ WHY DO IT?

To practice skip counting by twos, such as 2, 4, 6, 8
To show skip counting by twos with pictures

▦ HERE'S HOW!

1. Write out the numbers 1 through 20. Help the learner to circle every other number, that is 2, 4, 6, . . . 20. Have the learner say only the circled numbers.

1 2 3 4 5 6 7 8 9 10 11 12 13 14 15 16 17 18 19 20

2. Extend the activity by playing *Hide and Seek,* but count by twos while the learner is hiding.

▦ AN EASIER VARIATION:

Roll out clay or play dough and have the learner use two fingers to make ten pairs of fingerprints in the dough. Help count all the prints to 20 but whisper the odd numbers and emphasize the even numbers as 1,**2**,3,**4**,5,**6**,7,**8**,9,**10**,11,**12**, and so forth.

▦ AN ADVANCED VARIATION:

1. Have the learner skip count by twos up to 20. Help the learner if he needs it.
2. Have the learner discuss with you things that come in twos, for example, eyes, feet, and hands.
3. Have the learner choose items to either cut out or draw pictures of as in the example.

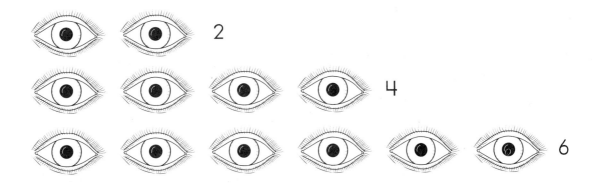

■ ANOTHER ADVANCED VARIATION:

1. Have the learner finish the twos chart with up to 50 (or more) to see if there is a pattern.

2	4	6	8	10
12	14	x	x	x
x	x	x	x	x
x	x	x	x	x
x	x	x	x	x

2. After he has discovered the patterns, cover up one number at a time by placing an object over it. Have the child tell what number is covered up.

Number Bowling

■ WHY DO IT?

To practice counting by ones, fives and/or other multiples

To practice making tally marks in groups of five

■ HERE'S HOW!

1. Collect ten quart-size milk cartons or ten tall juice cans and a ball.
2. Set the milk cartons or cans out like bowling pins.
3. Take turns with the learner trying to knock down the pins with the ball.
4. After each turn, help the learner count the number of pins he has knocked over. Write the tally marks in groups of five to keep score and have the child count them by 5s and 1s (as ||||| ||||| || = 5, 10, 11, 12).
5. The first player to reach 50 or some other agreed upon number wins.

■ AN EASIER VARIATION:

1. Use five milk cartons or juice cans for *each* player.
2. Take turns knocking down the pins with the ball.
3. Each player counts how many he knocked down after a turn.
4. After each turn match the pins side by side to see who has knocked down the most.

■ AN ALTERNATE VARIATION:

1. Provide the learners with "Give Me 5" verification certificates, such as the one below indicating books read, and then have them take part in any or all of the following activities.
2. For every 5 books that someone reads to the learner (or that he is able to read independently) fill out a slip like the one below. Then count by 5s all of the books read. (If this is done in school and the class reaches 100 books, a popcorn party might be given as a reward.)

"GIVE ME 5" BOOKS READ

Title _____

Title _____

Title _____

Title _____

Title _____

Signature_____

(Parent, Older Student, or Teacher)

3. Keep track of other things accomplished in groups of five such as chores completed or kind acts performed. Then count them in groups of five every day and do something special when the learner reaches a predetermined goal.

■ AN ADVANCED VARIATION:

1. Follow the directions for *Number Bowling*.
2. Modify directions to include making tally marks in groups of 3 or 4 or 6 or 7 and practice counting by these multiples.

More or Less

WHY DO IT?

To physically count and compare numbers of items
To deal with more and less relationships

HERE'S HOW!

1. Assemble a more and less spinner for this game (see Appendix A) and provide 10 items, such as beans, Lifesavers®, blocks, or small stones, for each player.
2. Have each player secretly put from 1 to 10 items in his or her hand and also secretly write that number.
3. Spin the spinner to see whether the player(s) who has *less* than a designated number wins that point.
4. Players then tell each other how many items they have, state whether they have *more* or *less,* and prove it by counting their objects.
5. The player who attains 5 points first is the winner.
6. If one or more of the players is ready for further *challenges,* increase the number of items to 15 or 20 and repeat the activity.

AN EASIER VARIATION:

1. Place two sets of items (buttons, beans, blocks) so that the learner may observe them.
2. Ask the learner to select either the set with *more* or the set with *less* items.
3. Ask how he determined this. The learner might count each set to prove his answer.

ANOTHER EASIER VARIATION:

1. Work with a learner or allow two learners to work together.
2. One player places a set of items on the table.
3. The second player spins the spinner to determine if he should provide a set with *more* or *less* items.
4. The second player then places a comparison set of objects on the table.
5. The first player then counts the items in both sets to check whether or not the second player is correct.

■ AN ADVANCED VARIATION:

1. Using a deck of cards (minus face cards and jokers) deal five cards to each player and turn up the top card from the pile.
2. To begin, flip a coin to indicate whether each player in turn must play a card that is *more* or *less* than the card turned up (Heads = *more* and Tails = *less*).
3. If a player does not have a playable card, he must draw from the stack until able to play.
4. If, however, the player has a card of the same value he may play that card and initiate a change in direction. For example, if a *more* card has been called for, but a player places a matching number card (such as an 8 on an 8) this forces a change in direction such that subsequent cards played must be *less*.
5. The first person to play all of his cards is the winner.

Cereal Count

WHY DO IT?

To gather, count, and illustrate data

To develop place value understandings for tens and ones

HERE'S HOW!

1. Use Cheerios® and Froot Loops® cereals together with a needle and thread (stiff or waxed string will work if you do not wish the learner to use a needle).
2. Have the learner count out 9 Cheerios and thread them onto the thread or string. Make the 10th piece a colored Froot Loop.
3. Add more Cheerios while counting 11, 12, 13, and so on, but stipulate that every 10th cereal piece must be a colored Froot Loop.
4. Continue to 21, 22, 23, and further so long as the learner appears to be understanding.

AN EASIER VARIATION:

1. Have the learner count a small number of individual breakfast cereal pieces.
2. Begin with 5 or 6 randomly placed Cheerios and note whether the learner uses a system that avoids counting the cereal pieces more than once (such as moving each piece apart as it is counted).
3. If successful, try the task again with 12 to 15 pieces and again with more than 20.
4. If a further *challenge* is desired, have the learner count larger numbers of Cheerios and put them in groupings of 10 as he does so.

AN ADVANCED VARIATION:

1. Have the learner make a long item, such as a necklace or belt with the Cheerios and Froot Loops.
2. She might make a string as tall as her height being certain that 9 pieces are Cheerios and the 10th piece is a colored Froot Loop.
3. When an item is finished have the learner count the cereal pieces by 10s and 1s. For example, a necklace might contain 53 cereal pieces and should be counted as 10, 20, 30, 40, 50, 51, 52, and 53.
4. Longer strings, such as those representing the height of a tall learner, will require counting to 100 and more.

Fraction Play Dough

■ WHY DO IT?

To practice hands-on experiences with basic fraction concepts

■ HERE'S HOW!

1. Help the learner make play dough (Use this Easy Play Dough recipe or see Appendix A for a Cooked Play Dough recipe).

Easy Play Dough

3 cups flour   3/4 cup salt   1/2 cup water
(optional) dry nontoxic tempera paint or 2 tsp. food coloring

(1) Sift flour and salt together into a pan. (2) Mix coloring with water and add gradually to flour and salt mixture. (3) Knead as you would bread dough until the mixture is smooth and easy to handle. The more the mixture is kneaded the smoother it becomes. (4) If mixture becomes sticky add more flour. (5) When not in use, place in a plastic bag and keep in a cool place. This Easy Play Dough should last for at least two weeks.

2. Have the learner make an object, such as a snake, and then divide it in halves. Ask how many halves there are? When he says 2, show how to write the fraction for each portion (half) as 1/2 and note that this means 1 out of 2 parts that are the same size.
3. Have the learner put the dough back together and make a different object. If a pancake is made, have the learner cut it into 2 parts of the same size. Point out that there had been one whole pancake and that it now has two equal portions; we say each part is one-half and is written as 1/2.
4. If the learner appears to understand the concept of a fraction, try making other objects and working with fourths (1 of 4 equal portions) or sixths, or eighths and indicate how the fraction is written (1/4, 1/6, 1/8).

■ AN EASIER VARIATION:

1. Read the book *Eating Fractions*[3] with the learners. Talk about how the children in the story divided food items.
2. Share a banana by cutting it into two equal portions (halves) as the children did in the book.
3. Share halves of other foods, such as one-half of a sandwich or one-half of an apple.
4. If the book *Eating Fractions* is unavailable, make up your own story about two children or a parent and a child who have only one of each food item and wish to share them.

■ AN ADVANCED VARIATION:

1. Have the learner divide a ball of play dough into halves. Is he sure the halves are equal?

2. Ask that one half be made into a long snake and the other half into a box shape.

3. Then ask whether the snake and the box shape are each made up of one-half of the dough? (Most young learners will insist that the halves do not contain the same amount of dough.)

4. Have the learner remake the box shape into a long snake and he may now agree that each snake is one-half of the play dough. (*Note:* Do not be overly concerned if the child doesn't *get it* at this time. With time and proper experiences, such as this task, he will master this concept.)

5. If the learner remains interested, try dividing the play dough in halves again and make other contrasting shapes such as a pancake and a ball or a fish and a ring.

6. At the conclusion of each trial have the learner mold each half back into the same shape so that he can see that the amount of play dough has not changed.

Underhand

WHY DO IT?

To use everyday objects to increase number sense
To begin to develop basic number combination understandings

HERE'S HOW!

1. Find small objects to work with such as beans or popcorn kernels or marbles. Have the learner count out a small number of the objects, perhaps 4.
2. Then, have the learner turn her back or cover her eyes while you cover up 0, 1, 2, 3, or all of the objects with your hand.
3. Have the learner look at the uncovered items and tell how many are under your hand. If, for example, 4 objects were used and only 1 is showing, the learner should say that 3 are under your hand.
4. If the learner is interested, keep a record of each trial. In the situation above the learner might draw a picture and/or write $1 + 3 = 4$. Also discuss and record $3 + 1 = 4$.

•   (• • •)

5. If the learner appears ready, try this Underhand activity with more objects such as 7 or 10 or 12 or even 20 or more.

AN EASIER VARIATION:

1. Have the learner count 4 to 7 randomly arranged objects and discern whether he can do so without missing items or counting some more than once.
2. If the learner has difficulty, help him by moving each object to the side once it has been counted.
3. If successful, repeat the task using greater numbers of objects.

AN ADVANCED VARIATION:

1. Have one player make a number combination with objects and have his or her partner try to figure out what it is.
2. For example, the first player might cover a number of marbles with his hand and leave 4 showing. He might then say, "I have 13 marbles altogether. Tell how many marbles are under my hand, draw a picture of this, and write equations that tell about this problem." The partner should answer that there are 9 marbles under his hand, and write the related equations as $4 + 9 = 13$, $9 + 4 = 13$, $13 - 4 = 9$ and $13 - 9 = 4$.

• • • •   (• • • • • • • • •)

Rocks in Hand

■ WHY DO IT?

To practice estimation and counting

■ HERE'S HOW!

1. Gather a bunch of small rocks (or you may use beans, peanuts, or macaroni).
2. One player grabs a handful of rocks.
3. All players estimate (guess) the number of rocks in that player's hand.
4. Count the rocks together. Help the learners compare the estimate with the actual number of rocks in that handful. (A learner who has the skills may subtract or add to find the difference.)

■ AN EASIER VARIATION:

1. Gather larger objects such as small blocks, tile pieces, or small toy cars.
2. Play the game as noted above, but when counting place the objects in a straight line so they can be easily viewed on a one-to-one basis.
3. Help the learners determine how close their estimate was to the actual number.

■ ANOTHER EASIER VARIATION:

1. Use objects such as rocks, pattern blocks, or tile pieces and play the game with two players.
2. Each player grabs a handful of rocks and counts them out.
3. Players then line up the rocks in lines that correspond one to one to see who has the most or least.

■ AN ADVANCED VARIATION:

1. Gather objects that are quite small, such as popcorn kernels or dried split peas.
2. Play the game as described, but when counting the actual number of popcorn kernels, have the learner place and count them in groups of tens and ones. (It may be necessary to count to 100 or more.)

Teen Recognition

■ WHY DO IT?

To recognize and name the numbers 11 through 19

To understand the quantity for the numbers 11 through 19 (the "teens")

To develop place value concepts

■ HERE'S HOW!

1. Provide a set of cards numbered 10 through 19 and a supply of straws or toothpicks and rubber bands or twist ties.
2. Count out ten straws, fasten them together as a bundle, and place the bundle on the 10 card. Next, count out 11 straws. Bundle 10 together and place that bundle plus the one extra straw on the 11 number card.
3. Continue this procedure until the learner has matched bundles and extras to all of the cards numbered 10 through 19.
4. If a further *challenge* is desired, make a set of cards numbered 20 through 29 and have the learner place the appropriate number of bundles and loose straws on each numbered card.

■ AN EASIER VARIATION:

1. Make a set of cards numbered 11 through 19 using index cards.
2. Talk about the names "eleven" through "nineteen" and help the learner put the cards in order and call out the names.
3. Ask the learner if she can see some ways in which the numbers 1 through 9 are like the numbers 11 through 19. (As a hint, have the learner look at the right-hand digit in each of the "teens" numbers.)

■ ANOTHER EASIER VARIATION:

1. Prepare two sets of cards numbered 11 through 19 and play a memory game.
2. Place all of the cards face down on a tabletop.
3. Have the learner try to find matching cards. When successful, have the learner place all of the cards in number order from 11 through 19.

■ AN ADVANCED VARIATION:

1. Assemble two "teen" dice (see making or modifying dice in Appendix A); one die should be numbered 11, 12, 13, 14, 15, and 16 and the other die 14, 15, 16, 17, 18, and 19. Photocopy the *Teen Recognition Game Board* and provide markers such as beans, buttons, nuts, or bolts for each player.

2. Each player begins on one of the black dots in the corners of the game board.

3. Each player in turn selects either the 11 through 16 or the 14 through 19 die and rolls it. He must identify the number on the die before moving his marker.

4. If the number is identified correctly, that player moves his marker one space horizontally, vertically, or diagonally to a matching teen number. If, however, the die does not match a number directly next to the player's marker, no move can be made.

5. Players take turns moving until someone reaches a center square. The person who reaches a center square first wins.

TEEN RECOGNITION GAME BOARD

●	13	15	17	18	14	16	●
16	14	19	13	15	11	15	18
15	17	13	14	16	17	18	14
13	12	17	15	18	14	13	17
15	14	18	13	16	17	14	11
16	17	15	14	15	18	13	15
13	18	16	17	13	19	16	14
●	15	12	18	14	15	18	●

Fraction Plates

■ WHY DO IT?

To provide hands-on and visual experiences with basic fraction concepts

■ HERE'S HOW!

1. Obtain inexpensive paper plates (or substitute paper squares or coffee filters) that may be marked on and cut up.
2. Have the learner mark 1 on a plate for one whole amount.
3. Being as accurate as possible, draw a line through the center of a second plate and use scissors to cut along this line. Ask how many parts there are after it has been cut and whether the parts are the same size.
4. Since there are now 2 equal segments, a 2 should be written on each part and a 1 above each 2. This tells the learner that each portion is 1 of 2 equal parts. We usually call each part one-half or a half.
5. Continue this process with another plate being cut into fourths (with each portion being 1 of 4 equal parts). These plates will be enough to begin, but as the learner appears ready, additional plates may be cut into eighths, thirds, sixths, and so forth.
6. Have the learner use the plates to explore fraction equivalence concepts. Ask, for example, how many of the 1/2 pieces are the same as the 1 whole plate and have the learner prove his or her result by physically matching a 1/2 plate plus another 1/2 plate to the 1 whole plate.
7. As the learner is doing the matching you might keep a record by writing down 1/2 + 1/2 = 2/2 = 1 and pointing out to the learner how this is related to the matching of the paper plate fractions.
8. As this process continues the learner should be able to match and discover 1/4 + 1/4 + 1/4 + 1/4 = 4/4 = 1 and 1/4 + 1/4 = 2/4 = 1/2, and so forth.

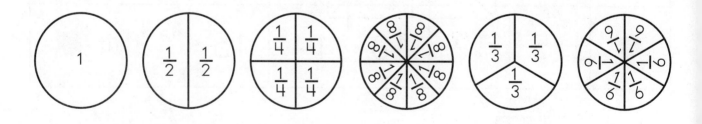

■ AN EASIER VARIATION:

1. To play *Cut and Eat a Cookie,* soft cookies and a table knife are needed.
2. Have the learner cut a cookie into 2 parts of the same size and ask how many cookies he started with and how many parts there are after cutting.

3. Discuss the fact that we usually call each part a half, but that each is really 1 of 2 equal pieces.
4. If the learner knows her numbers you might write 1/2 next to each cookie part and again note that each half is 1 of 2 equal pieces.
5. Then allow the learner to eat 1/2 of the cookie and perhaps the other half too.
6. Continue by having the learner cut another cookie into 4 parts of the same size and discuss the idea that each 1/4 is 1 of 4 equal pieces.

■ AN ADVANCED VARIATION:

1. Have two or more players try the fraction game *Cover One Whole.*
2. Each player will need a whole paper plate. Also needed are fraction pieces cut and labeled as follows: one each of the 1/2, 1/3, and 1/4 sizes and four each for sizes 1/6, 1/8, and 1/16 and a spinner marked with the same fraction values (see instructions for a Paper Clip Spinner in Appendix A).
3. At each turn a player spins a fraction and chooses whether or not to place the corresponding fractional part on his or her own plate. The object is to put together a set of fractional pieces that will exactly *cover* their *one whole* plate. (In the example below Player #1 needs a 1/8, whereas Player #2 could win with a 1/4, or with 1/8 + 1/8, or with 1/8 + 1/16 + 1/16, or with four 1/16th pieces.)

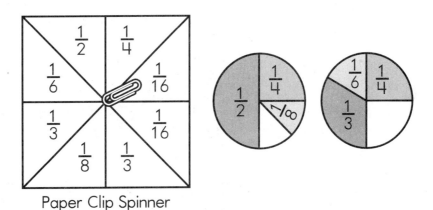

Paper Clip Spinner

Birthday List

WHY DO IT?

To recognize numbers and their uses in daily life

To place nonsequential numbers in numerical order

HERE'S HOW!

1. Have the learner ask the birthdays of friends and family members.
2. Using only the day of the month, help the learner write the dates on index cards and order them between 1 and 31. (*Note:* Some family members may have the same date but in different months.)

AN EASIER VARIATION:

1. Give the learner two nonsequential number cards, such as 6 and 2, and ask him to put them in numerical order from least to most.
2. As the learner feels comfortable, increase the number of cards until he can sequence all of the numbers from 1 through 9.

ANOTHER EASIER VARIATION:

1. Deal a set of playing cards (remove face cards and joker) to two, three, or four players.
2. Each player places his or her cards in a pile with the numbers facing down. Then each player turns over and shows the card from the top of his or her pile.
3. The player with the highest number gets all the cards. In case of a tie each player plays a second card from his or her pile.

S	M	T	W	T	F	S
1	2	3	4	5	6	7
8	9	10	11	12	13	14
15	16	17	18	19	20	21
22	23	24	25	26	27	28
29	30	31				

S	M	T	W	T	F	S
		1	2	3	4	5
6	7	8	9	10	11	12
13	14	15	16	17	18	19
20	21	22	23	24	25	26
27	28	29	30	31		

■ AN ADVANCED VARIATION:

1. Look at a calendar and talk about the order of months, that is, January is the first month of the year, and so forth, and the number of days in each month.
2. Have the child mark the birthdays of each family member on the family calendar.

■ A MORE ADVANCED VARIATION:

1. Photocopy enough calendar pages so that each learner may make her or his own year-long calendar.
2. Help each learner to note and number the days in each month.
3. Have each learner indicate family birthdays, observed holidays, and other planned events throughout the year.
4. As a creative experience the learner might draw a picture for each month.

■ ANOTHER ADVANCED VARIATION:

1. Have the learner note the different ways in which dates are written.
2. Note, for example, that the most common practice in the United States is to denote month/date/year, such as January 23, 1999 or 1/23/99.
3. However, in some parts of the world the date is generally written first as 23 January 1999. Discuss these conventions with the learner noting why they are written as such.

Sunday	Monday	Tuesday	Wednesday	Thursday	Friday	Saturday

Order Race

■ WHY DO IT?

To practice arranging the numbers 1 through 31 in numerical order

■ HERE'S HOW!

1. Help the learner cut number boxes from an old calendar month with 31 days. Mix up the pieces and encourage the learner to reorder them from 1 through 31 .
2. Mix the calendar pieces again and keep track of the time it takes the learner to put them in order. Repeat and see if he can do it faster.
3. If competition is desired, cut out two sets of calendar numbers and have two players *race* to see who can put them in numerical order first.

S	M	T	W	T	F	S
1	2	3	4	5	6	7
8	9	10	11	12	13	14
15	16	17	18	19	20	21
22	23	24	25	26	27	28
29	30	31				

■ AN EASIER VARIATION:

1. Use two old calendar pages, each with 31 days. Cut one apart.
2. Ask the learner to match numbers. He should do so by placing each of the cut out numbers on top of the corresponding number on the uncut calendar page.
3. Finish by having the learner orally count the days.

■ AN ADVANCED VARIATION:

1. Place the numbers 1 through 31 in a container.
2. Have the learner draw out two numbers and identify the larger number.
3. As an alternate format, have two players each draw a number and determine who has the larger number.

■ ANOTHER ADVANCED VARIATION:

1. Ask the learner to place the numerals in reverse (backward) order as 31, 30, 29, and so forth.
2. If successful, ask that she also orally say them in reverse order. (*Note:* This is a task that some young learners may not yet be able to perform.)

■ A MORE ADVANCED VARIATION:

1. Using only the numbers from 1 through 9, have the learner draw two numbers and place them together to form a two-digit number.
2. Ask the learner to identify that number.
3. Then ask him to reverse the two numbers and identify the new number.
4. Finally, ask which is the larger number?

Counting with Glasses

■ WHY DO IT?

To gather items and count them by 1s, 10s, and so forth

To develop place value understanding

■ HERE'S HOW!

1. Help the learner to find and count a large number of drinking glasses or paper cups. Have the learner place them on a table or countertop in groups of 10. For example, if 23 glasses are found, the learner should arrange them as 2 groups of ten and 3 groups of one.
2. Have the learner draw a simple picture or diagram showing the arrangement of the glasses.
3. Write the numeral for the total number of glasses on top of the page and discuss the meaning of the 10s and 1s in this number with the learner.
4. Additionally, ask the learner to count other objects, such as light bulbs, paper clips, or cookies in a package, and relate them as groups of 10s and 1s.

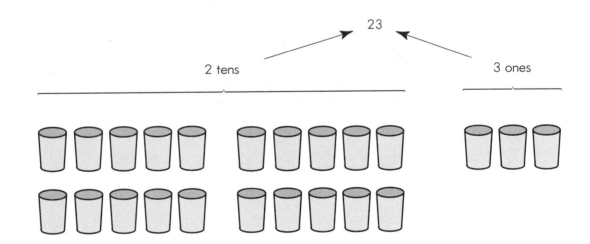

■ AN EASIER VARIATION:

1. Begin by having the learner count 5 to 8 randomly arranged glasses and note whether he avoids counting some of the glasses more than once.
2. If the learner finds this difficult, show her how moving each glass to the side once it has been counted can be a help.
3. If successful, have the learner do the task again with more than 10 glasses, and again with more than 20.

■ AN ADVANCED VARIATION:

1. Use small objects such as raisins, Cheerios®, or paper clips and several stackable drinking glasses. Have the learner count out 24 raisins and place them so there are 10 raisins in each glass with any extra raisins remaining on the tabletop.

2. Count them as 10, 20, 21, 22, 23, and 24. Continue this activity with more and more raisins, making certain the learner understands the process of counting by 10s and 1s.

3. When the learner attains 100 items have the glasses (with 10 raisins in each) stacked 10 high and begin counting and using place value for 100s, 10s and 1s. For example, 123 or 100 + 20 + 3 is shown below.

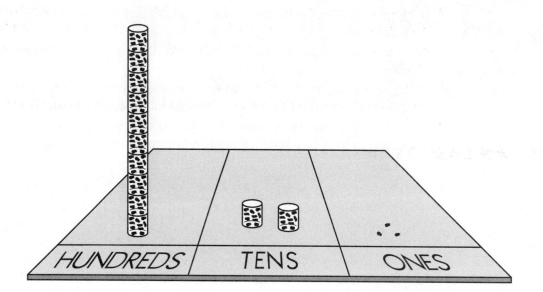

Finding Fractions

■ WHY DO IT?

To learn to see common fractions in different shapes and sizes

■ HERE'S HOW!

1. Help the learner search for fractional things at home or in the classroom. For example, if the concept of one-half is to be explored, look around the house, especially the kitchen, and help the learner find something that illustrates this concept.
2. Have the learner share the halves with someone else. For example, he might show two halves of an apple, the halves of a large cookie, a half loaf of bread, or one-half of a puzzle. Note that we commonly call each one-half, but this really means 1 of 2 equal parts which is written as 1/2.
3. If the task with halves was enjoyable, have the learner try to locate things that come in 1/4ths (1 of 4 equal parts) or 1/3rds (1 of 3 equal parts), and so forth.

■ AN EASIER VARIATION:

1. Point out to the learner some things that are halves. Note that we say half and write it as 1/2 which means 1 of 2 parts that are the same size.
2. Work together to find examples and make a list of the things found such as 1/2 of an orange, a sheet of paper folded to show halves, 1/2 of a piece of toast, or 1/2 of a carrot. (*Note:* the list will need to be in picture form for young learners.)

■ AN ADVANCED VARIATION:

1. A learner who is ready might try dealing with a fraction of a group.
2. As such she might be presented with 4 pieces of candy and asked how many make up half. (Remember that 1/2 means 1 of 2 equal parts.) As such the learner might be asked to place equal amounts in each of 2 bowls.
3. Try the task again, but this time with 8 pieces of candy, or 6 pieces of candy, or 10 pieces of candy. Help the learner to notice that in each case, even though the number of pieces of candy varies, there are always 2 equal groups.

Right On/Before/After Roll

■ WHY DO IT?

To practice place value

To recognize numbers that come before and after

■ HERE'S HOW!

1. Construct dice with the numbers 0 through 5 on one and 1 through 6 on the other (see Appendix A for instructions on how to make or modify dice) and different markers, such as buttons, paper clips, or beans, for each player.
2. To begin playing *Right On,* the first player rolls the dice and arranges them as a two-digit number. For example, for 2 and 5 the player could make 25 and say twenty-five or he could make 52 and say fifty-two.
3. After correctly saying the number aloud that player places his marker in the corresponding spot on the game board. (See the *Right On/Before/After Game Board.*)
4. The game ends when each of the players cannot place a marker on the game board. For example, if a player rolls a 3 and a 4 and both 43 and 34 are covered, he must stop. The other players may continue until they are also unable to play. When the game ends, the players should each count up the total number of spaces they were able to cover and say and write that total.

■ AN EASIER VARIATION:

1. Play the game as noted above, but, in addition to saying the number rolled and finding the proper place on the game board, also use straws and rubber bands to physically show the numbers.
2. If, for example, 32 is rolled, have the learner build it as three bundles of 10 straws each held together with rubber bands plus 2 loose straws. Then help the learner to see that she has 3 bundles which equal 30 and 2 more straws so there are 32 straws in all.

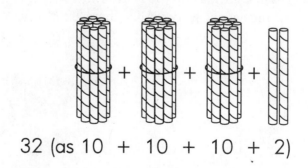

32 (as 10 + 10 + 10 + 2)

■ AN ADVANCED VARIATION:

1. Construct dice with the numbers 0 through 5 on one and 1 through 6 on the other (Appendix A contains instructions on how to make or modify dice) and find different markers such as buttons, beans, nuts, bolts, or small stones for each player.

2. To begin playing *Before and After* a player rolls the dice and chooses one number to put in the tens place and the other in the ones place. For example, if a 3 and a 5 are rolled, the player could choose to make either a 35 or a 53.

3. The player may then choose the number that is before or after the rolled number, name it, and place a single marker on the game board. For example, if 35 is chosen, the marker could be placed on either 34 or 36. If 53 is designated, then either 54 or 52 must be marked.

4. If all possible numbers are already covered, that player does not cover any number and forfeits his turn.

5. When the entire game board is covered, or a specified time has elapsed, the player with the most markers on the board wins.

6. As a *challenge,* adept players may be allowed to put as many markers on the board as possible in one turn. For example, if they roll a 3 and a 5, they may put markers on 34, 36, 52, and 54 if not already covered.

RIGHT ON/BEFORE/AFTER GAME BOARD

1	2	3	4	5	6	7	8
9	10	11	12	13	14	15	16
17	18	19	20	21	22	23	24
25	26	27	28	29	30	31	32
33	34	35	36	37	38	39	39
41	42	43	44	45	46	47	48
49	50	51	52	53	54	55	56
57	58	59	60	61	62	63	64

65	66

Closer Is Better

■ WHY DO IT?

To further develop place value understandings

■ HERE'S HOW!

1. Use the ace through 5 cards from a deck of regular playing cards (or make your own set of cards with four of each card numbered 1 through 5).
2. Shuffle the cards and deal three to each player.
3. Place the remaining cards face down in the center of the play area.
4. Turn up the first two cards from the center pile to obtain the target number. The first card turned up is the tens place and the second card is the ones place. For example, if the first card is a 2 and the second is a 6, the target number is 26.
5. Each player then decides which two cards in his or her hand to keep to make a number as near as possible to the target number. The third card in each hand is discarded.
6. Each player shows and says the number in his or her hand. Which player has the closest number? Ask the players to determine this by making physical representations of each number. To do so the players might bundle straws in groups of tens and ones using rubber bands. Then use the appropriate number of bundles and single straws to represent the target number and the number of each player.

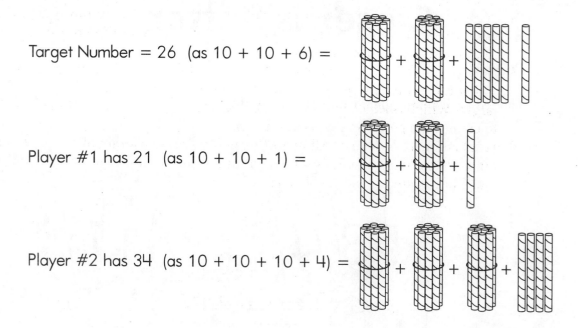

Target Number = 26 (as 10 + 10 + 6) =

Player #1 has 21 (as 10 + 10 + 1) =

Player #2 has 34 (as 10 + 10 + 10 + 4) =

7. If the players are interested in keeping score, grant a point for the player who is closest to the target number for each hand. The first player to reach five points wins.

■ AN EASIER VARIATION:

1. Play a game of *Show Me the Number*. Review the idea of place value by reminding the learner that two-digit numbers (anything over 9) have a tens column and a ones column. Have available bundles of ten straws rubber-banded together and single straws.
2. Use only the ace through 3 of a regular set of playing cards or make four sets of cards with the numbers 1 through 3 written on them. Ask the learner to turn over two cards. As the first card is turned over, say, "The 3 is in the tens column." When the second card is turned, say, "The 2 is in the ones column. The number is 32." Help the learner identify several more two-place numbers as she turns over cards.
3. After a selected number has been identified, help the learner to show that number with bundles of tens and loose straws as shown below.

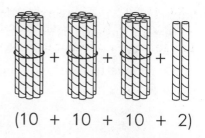

(10 + 10 + 10 + 2)

4. Without removing the first set of numbers and the matching straw representation, ask the learner to turn over another set of cards and repeat the process. Continue this activity until the learner feels confident.

5. Now you may want to add a *challenge.* Allow the learner to compare numbers by lining up and counting the bundles of tens and ones for each. Which number is larger? Which is smaller? As further proof, undo the bundles and allow the learner to count each group of straws one by one.

6. Want another *challenge*? Allow the learner to line up a group of 13 straws and another of 18 straws one under the other in a 1-to-1 fashion. Then count how many more straws are in the line of 18 straws.

$$13 \text{ (as } 10 + 3) =$$

$$18 \text{ (as } 10 + 8) =$$

◼ AN ADVANCED VARIATION:

1. Play the game as explained in the original variation above but work with three-digit numbers, including the hundreds column. Use ace through 9 from a regular card deck (or make your own set of cards with four of each number from 1 through 9) and deal 4 cards to each player.

2. Allow each player to arrange three cards to make a number as near the target as possible and discard the fourth card. Which player has the number nearest in value to the target number?

3. Ask the players to show the difference between their number and the target number by subtracting and/or using bundles and loose straws.

4. As a *challenge,* the learner might also draw pictures or diagrams to illustrate the problem. For example, if the target number is 238 and the student draws cards for 259, he might show his number using a dot diagram as shown.

259 =

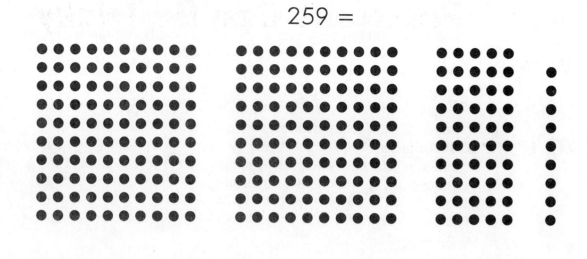

238 =

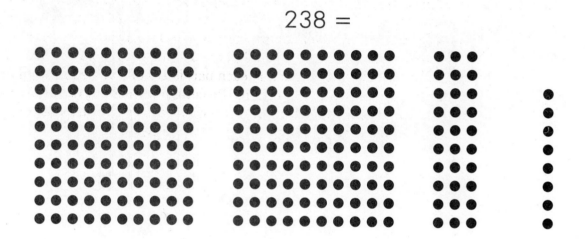

(See Appendix A for dot paper that may be photocopied.)

Fractions Can Be Tricky

■ WHY DO IT?

To provide a variety of experiences with everyday fraction concepts

■ HERE'S HOW!

Fractions can be experienced in a number of settings such as 1/2 gallon of milk, 1/2 of a group of 8 people = 4 people, 1/2 dollar = 50¢, or 1/2 of an apple. With this in mind the following everyday fraction experiences are suggested; try these and others that you are familiar with.

1. *Paper Folding.* Begin with four paper squares of the same dimensions (typing paper cut to size works well). Have the learner write 1 on the first square, which will serve as 1 whole amount. A second square needs 1 fold and each portion is labeled 1/2 (each is 1 of 2 equal parts). Another of the paper squares should have 2 folds (see diagram) such that each part is 1/4 or 1 of 4 equal segments. Finally a third fold will yield 1/8 portions. Be certain to spend time discussing these fraction meanings with the learner. Try a similar activity with paper circles (*Note:* Circles might also be folded as sixths or twelfths.)

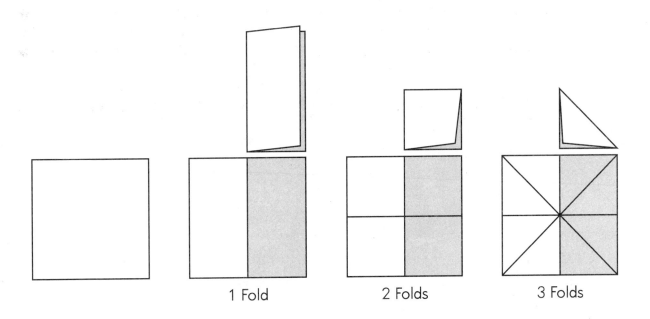

1 Fold   2 Folds   3 Folds

2. *Repeating Figure Fractions.* Designate a geometric shape as a basic fraction and then have the learner demonstrate how the whole figure might appear. For example, in the illustration below the triangle is designated as 1/4 and possible solutions are

shown. The learner's thinking might be extended by designating the same triangle as 1/6; then what might be possible outcomes? What might happen if triangles of other dimensions are used? Or squares? Or rectangles?

If this piece is one-fourth, make a whole.

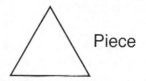

Possible Solutions

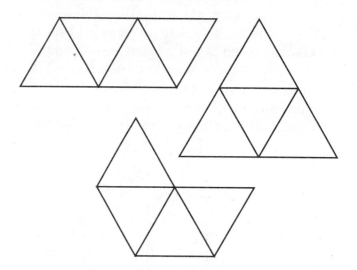

3. *Half Full.* Containers of the following sizes will be needed: gallon, half gallon, quart, pint, and cup (one-half pint). Allow the learner to experiment by pouring water (or a dry material such as uncooked rice) from one container to another. Then ask leading questions such as: How many cups does it take to fill the pint jar? If 2 cups fill it, how many will make it 1/2 full? So, is a cup 1/2 of a pint? Explain it to me. How many pint jars fill the quart container? So what fraction of a quart is the pint? Can you explain it to me? Now a harder question. How many cups does it take to fill the quart container? Try it and find out. If 4 cups fill it, what fraction of the quart is each cup? Explain it to me. Continue with such pouring activities and the related questions so long as the learner does not get frustrated. If the learner does not yet *get it,* please don't be overly concerned. With proper experiences, such as those noted here, and as the learner gets older the expected understanding will come.

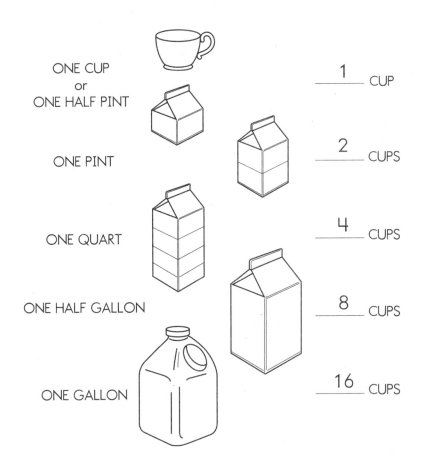

ONE CUP
or
ONE HALF PINT

ONE PINT

ONE QUART

ONE HALF GALLON

ONE GALLON

___1___ CUP

___2___ CUPS

___4___ CUPS

___8___ CUPS

___16___ CUPS

4. *Berry Pies.* Fractions dealing with groups of things are often difficult for learners to understand; as such, this activity may be helpful. Paper plates or circles that may be drawn on and about 20 objects of the same kind (for example, berries, pennies, or paper clips) are needed for this activity. Begin with a paper plate that has a line drawn through the center and perhaps 12 berries. Have the learner place an equal number of berries in each piece of the pie. Then have the learner describe what happened. The learner might be prompted to explain that each piece is 1/2 of the pie and there are 6 berries in each. So, 1/2 of the 12 is 6 berries. Have the learner do similar activities with pies that have been cut into fractional pieces of varying sizes and with different numbers of berries. Some possibilities are shown below.

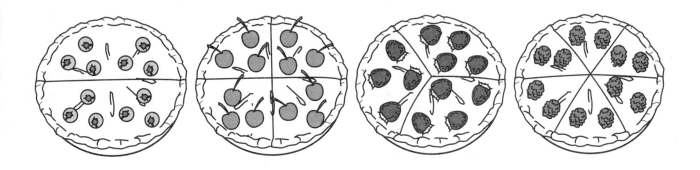

Works Cited

1. Roger Hargreaves, *Count Worm* (Miami, Florida: P.S.I. & Associates, Ottenheimer Publishers, 1982).
2. Pat Hutchins, *The Doorbell Rang* (New York: William Morrow, 1986).
3. Bruce McMillan, *Eating Fractions* (New York: Scholastic, 1991).

CHAPTER 2

Number Operations

The activities in this chapter will help learners to comprehend more than just how to *do* addition and subtraction. The learners will be encouraged to use manipulatives, visual aids, estimation, and to talk about their thinking as they work toward answers. Because they will understand the meaning of the operations, learners will have little trouble mastering basic facts. An added bonus is that these activities will be used in an atmosphere of fun and, as such, rich mathematical conversations will result between parents and children and between teachers and children.

63

Combinations in the Hand

WHY DO IT?

To practice number combinations

To develop logical reasoning skills

HERE'S HOW!

1. Provide several small objects (perhaps five) such as beans, stones, or buttons.
2. One player holds some of the five objects in one hand and the remainder in the other hand so that both amounts may be seen by a second player.
3. The other player writes down a number sentence showing how many are in each hand. If, for example, there are three stones in one hand and two stones in the other, the number sentence would be 3 + 2 = 5. (*Note:* If writing the sentence is too difficult, have the learner tell in his or her own words what the situation is. Then you or an older student might write the equation.)
4. Have the first player rearrange the stones so there is a different amount in each hand. Then say and write another number sentence that equals five.
5. How many different number sentences can you make that equal five? What happens if you put all the objects in one hand and none in the other?
6. Try this activity again with a different number of objects.

AN EASIER VARIATION:

1. Place a small number of objects such as beans, perhaps three, on a tabletop and have the learner count them.
2. Have the learner cover all of the beans with his hand. Then ask how many objects are under the hand.
3. Ask the learner to cover some but not all of the beans. Ask how many can be seen and how many are under the hand? Have the learner tell a story about the situation. For example, if two beans are under the hand and one is showing, the child might say, "One bean is showing and I have two more under my hand, so there are three beans in all."
4. When successful, try the activity again with different numbers of objects.

AN ADVANCED VARIATION:

1. Get several (perhaps six) small objects such as beans, pebbles, or buttons.
2. Player #1 holds some of the objects in an open hand and the remainder in the other hand, which is closed.

3. Player #2 looks at the objects in the open hand and tries to figure out how many are in the closed hand. She then says how many are in the closed hand, checks to see if she is correct, and writes the number sentence to match.

4. Continue by rearranging the same six objects together so that there is a different amount in each hand. Then repeat direction number 3. If capable, the player might also write a missing addend equation; for example, if two beans are showing and it is known that six is the total, then the player might write $2 + \Delta = 6$.

5. Try the activity again using five or more objects.

Cover That Number

■ WHY DO IT?

To enhance number recognition skills

To practice addition facts to ten

To develop logical thinking skills

■ HERE'S HOW!

1. Provide two 0 through 5 dice (see Appendix A for directions on how to make or modify dice), a number line from 0 through 10 for each player, and small objects (pennies, beans or popcorn) for use as markers.
2. To begin play, the first player rolls the dice and may cover either the sum of the two dice combined or the individual numbers from each die. If, for example, a player rolls a **4** and a **1** he may cover either the **5** or both the **4** and the **1.**
3. Following the same procedure the game continues with each player taking a turn. (If a player cannot use the numbers rolled, he or she must pass.)
4. The first person to cover all the numbers on his or her number line wins.

0	1	2	3	4	Δ	6	7	8	9	10

(Player #1 rolled a 4 and a 1. He decided to cover the 5.)

0	1	2	●	4	●	6	7	8	9	10

(Player #2 rolled a 3 and a 5. She decided to cover both 3 and 5.)

■ AN EASIER VARIATION:

1. Provide two 0 through 5 dice (see Appendix A), a number line from 0 through 10 and an object for use as a marker (a penny, bean, or paper clip).
2. The player begins by rolling the dice and orally identifying the numbers.
3. She then selects one of the numbers rolled, says what it is, and "hops" the marker from 0 to the matching number position on the number line.

4. Continuing from that matching number position, the player again hops the marker the number of times specified on the second die. If, for example, the numbers rolled are 5 and 2, the learner might hop the marker from 0 to 5 and then from 5 to 6 to 7.
5. Finally the player should identify the *answer* number and explain how she got there.

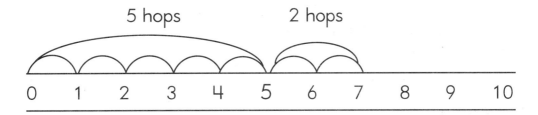

■ ANOTHER EASY VARIATION:

1. Provide a 6 × 6 grid, a different colored crayon for each player, and two 0 through 5 dice.
2. Help the players to randomly write the numbers 0 to 5 in grid boxes or photocopy the number grid provided.
3. In turn, each player rolls the dice, identifies those numbers, and uses his or her crayon to color in one matching grid box for each number rolled. If no number can be found, the player must pass.
4. When all numbers are colored the game ends. If a winner is desired, the player with the most numbers colored wins the game.

5	4	1	2	4	3
3	2	3	5	5	5
1	0	2	4	0	1
2	3	0	3	4	3
0	5	1	2	3	4
4	2	4	3	5	2

AN ADVANCED VARIATION:

1. Have each player roll the dice and identify the numbers.
2. He must then write those numbers as an addition or subtraction problem together with the answer on a magic slate, chalk board, or paper.

ANOTHER ADVANCED VARIATION:

1. The learner is to roll two dice and write and solve that addition number sentence. He should repeat this procedure nine more times. (*Note:* The number sentences might initially be written on small pieces of paper so they can be easily moved around.)
2. Then help the learner to develop a chart that shows the different number combinations that yield the same sum (a partial example is shown below). It is important to note that, for a beginner, $2 + 3 = 5$ is a very different number combination from $3 + 2 = 5$.)

1	2	3	4	etc.
$1 + 0 = 1$	$0 + 2 = 2$	$0 + 3 = 3$	$0 + 4 = 4$	
$0 + 1 = 1$	$2 + 0 + 2$	$3 + 0 = 3$	$4 + 0 = 4$	
	$1 + 1 = 2$	$1 + 2 = 3$	$1 + 3 = 4$	
		$2 + 1 = 3$	$3 + 1 = 4$	
			$2 + 2 = 4$	

Rolling Math Beans

■ WHY DO IT?

To help visualize math in a concrete manner

To practice counting and simple addition

To explore beginning probability

■ HERE'S HOW!

1. Make one or two dozen "math beans." To do so spread a single layer of large dried lima beans in a low-sided box and spray paint one side of the beans with a bright color (red or blue). Wait until dry and then spray the opposite side of each bean a contrasting color (green or yellow). You can also use contrasting permanent felt markers to do the coloring.
2. Provide each learner with five math beans, a small paper cup, crayons that match the colored sides of the beans, and a recording sheet.
3. Have the learner shake the beans and toss them on a flat surface.
4. She should then count the number of beans that are of one color, the number that are of a contrasting color, and orally state the results. For example, she might say, "I have three red beans and two green beans so 3 plus 2 makes 5."
5. Ask the learner to color in the recording sheet with the appropriate number of beans of each color and write the corresponding equation, such as 3 + 2 = 5. (To check for accuracy the student might actually place the beans on top those that she has colored in on the recording sheet.)

■ AN EASIER VARIATION:

1. Place ten math beans in a small container.
2. Ask the learner to shake and toss them on a flat surface.
3. Separate the beans into two groups according to color (red in one group, green in another).
4. Have the learner count the number of beans of each color and orally state the results. He might have, for example, four red beans and six green beans.
5. Ask whether there are more red beans or green beans. (*Note:* The learner may check by placing them in a one-to-one relationship on a grid like the one shown below.)
6. Repeat this activity several times and discuss the different number combinations.

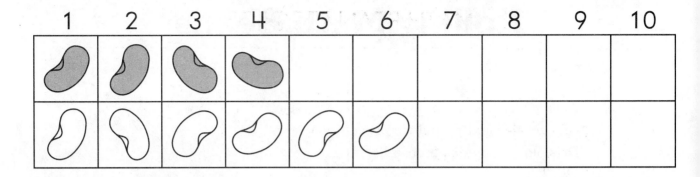

AN ADVANCED VARIATION:

1. Ask each learner to count out ten math beans and place them in a paper cup.
2. The learner should shake the cup, toss the beans onto a flat surface and count the number of beans that land with one color up and the number of beans with a contrasting color showing.
3. Have the learner write a corresponding addition equation such as 4 + 6 = 10. (*Note:* If this is too difficult, ask the learner to color in the number of beans of each color on the recording sheet and then help her to count and write the related equation.)
4. Repeat the activity ten times and note the variety of arrangements.
5. As a further *challenge,* ask the learner to determine how many different equations are possible when using 10 beans.

ANOTHER ADVANCED VARIATION:

1. Have the learner count out five math beans and place them in a paper cup.
2. Ask the learner to predict how many beans will land with the *red* side up when the math beans are tossed onto a flat surface.
3. He should then toss the beans and check his prediction. Repeat the activity several times and discuss the results.
4. As a further *challenge,* increase the number of math beans to ten, repeat the experiment ten or twenty times, and discuss whether certain outcomes are more likely than others.

MATH BEAN RECORDS

Get Ten

■ WHY DO IT?

To practice number combinations to 10

To encourage mental math thinking

■ HERE'S HOW!

1. The *Get Ten* game is played by pairs of learners (or a learner and an adult).
2. Each player draws 5 circles approximately 2 inches in diameter on a piece of paper and writes one number in each circle from the selection 9, 8, 7, 6, 5, or 4.
3. The players then take turns rolling a die. If a rolled number can be added to one of that player's circles to make 10, then she can draw an *X* in that circle. (*Note:* If a rolled number goes with a circle that has already been marked out, that player must pass and it becomes the other player's turn.)
4. The winner is the first player to be able to cross off all of her circles.

■ AN EASIER VARIATION:

1. This version is also played by pairs of learners who each draw five circles, but the numbers written in the circles must be 1, 2, 3, 4, 5, or 6.
2. The players then take turns rolling a die. If the number of dots on a rolled die matches a player's circled number he may mark it with an *X*. (*Note:* As in the original game, if a rolled number goes with a circle that has already been marked out, that player must pass and it becomes the other player's turn.)
3. The winner is the first player to be able to cross off all of his circles.

■ AN ADVANCED VARIATION:

1. Have the pairs of learners (or a learner and an adult) play a game of *Get Twenty*.
2. Each player draws 10 circles approximately 2 inches in diameter on a piece of paper and writes one number in each from the selection 8, 9, 10, 11, 12, 13, 14, 15, 16, 17, or 18.
3. The players then take turns rolling two dice. If the rolled numbers can be added to one of that player's circles to make 20, then she can draw an *X* in that circle. (*Note:* If the rolled numbers go with a circle that has already been marked out, that player must pass and it becomes the other player's turn.)
4. The winner is the first player to be able to cross off all of her circles.
5. As a further *challenge,* modify *Get Ten* or *Get Twenty* so that either may be played for subtraction.

Add 'Em and Eat 'Em

■ WHY DO IT?

To practice addition skills

To develop and/or reinforce an understanding of place value

■ HERE'S HOW!

1. Select edible items that the players may collect, count, and eat such as popcorn, cereal, raisins, or minimarshmallows.
2. Each player chooses a marker and places it on the *Add 'Em and Eat 'Em Game Board*.
3. In turn, each player rolls two 1-6 dice (see Appendix A for directions on making or modifying dice), adds up the numbers showing, and moves his marker that number of spaces. He then counts out treats equal to that total number and saves them.
4. The game continues until each player reaches the end. Once he has done so, have him place his items in groups of 10 and then count them as 10, 20, 30, and so forth. (this will help to reinforce place value concepts). When finished the players may eat their treats

■ AN EASIER VARIATION:

1. Help the learner make a set of cards having 1 to 5 dots or stickers on each. Allow the learner to select an edible item that she will be able to count, collect, and eat as her prize (Cheerios®, popcorn, raisins, M&Ms®).
2. Place the cards face down on a table. The learner then turns a card over, places an edible item on each dot or sticker, and counts the number of edible items that were placed on it.
3. The child may then eat the prize.

■ AN ADVANCED VARIATION:

1. Play an extended *Add 'Em and Eat 'Em* game where the players may accumulate large numbers of items. When doing so use cereal such as Cheerios® or Froot Loops®. Suggest optional uses for the edible items including: (1) adding milk and eating the Cheerios or Froot Loops; (2) stringing them to make necklaces or bird feeding strings (by making every tenth piece a colored Froot Loop place value will be reinforced).

ADD 'EM AND EAT 'EM GAME BOARD

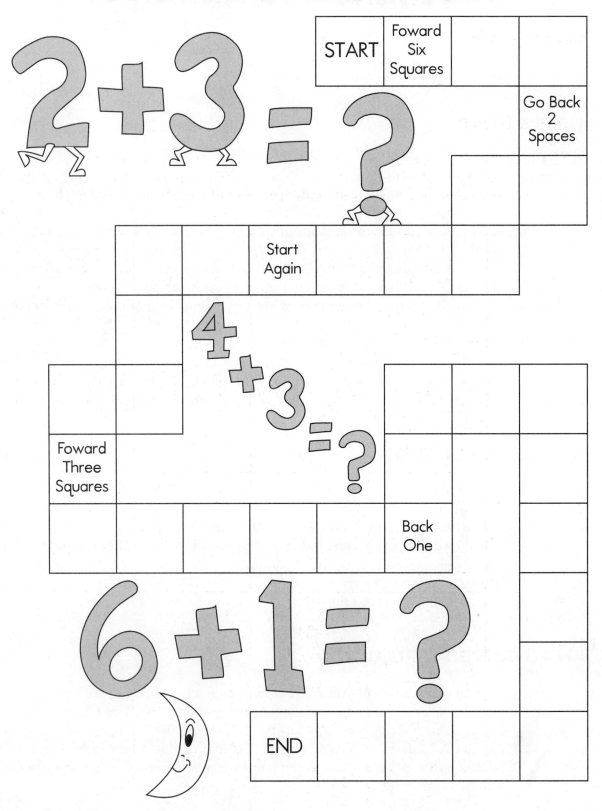

Animal Adoption

◼ WHY DO IT?

To use picture manipulatives to practice subtraction

◼ HERE'S HOW!

1. Photocopy the animal pictures shown and have the learners color and cut them out. Each player should then place the same number of animals (perhaps 10) in front of himself or herself. Also, provide a die numbered 1 through 6.

2. The players take turns saying, "I have ten animals (or the number of animals in front of them) to find homes for." Player #1 then rolls the die and says, "Four people (or whichever number appears on the die) want to adopt animals." She then takes that number of animals away and says, "Now I have six animals (the number remaining) that still need homes."
3. Player #2 continues in the same manner.
4. The first player to find homes for all of his or her animals wins.

■ AN EASIER VARIATION:

1. Give each player 6 beads and yarn and provide a 1 through 6 die.
2. Have the players string all six beads on their yarn. The first player then rolls the die, takes off the number of beads indicated, and states the related number sentence. If, for example, the player rolls a 2 then he might say, "Six minus two equals four," or "6 beads take away 2 beads leaves 4 beads." (*Note:* If this is too hard for the players, repeat that segment of the activity, talk about it, and then practice saying the number sentence together.)
3. After all players have had a turn, compare the number of beads left on their bead strings. Discuss who has the most left? The least?
4. Have the players restring their 6 beads and play again.

■ AN ADVANCED VARIATION:

1. Write a subtraction problem on the board or a piece of paper.
2. Have individual learners or small groups of learners tell an animal story to go along with the subtraction problem.
3. Repeat the story and have the learners act it out with animal manipulatives as it is being told. (Photocopy and cut out the animal pictures shown.)
4. As a further *challenge,* the learners might draw pictures to go along with their stories. When the pictures are complete, put them in a book with their matching subtraction equations on top of each page.

Above, Below, In, Left, Right

WHY DO IT?

To develop positional vocabulary and related listening skills

To practice basic fact computation

To enhance mental math abilities

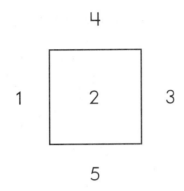

HERE'S HOW!

1. Use the box and numbers as shown or draw a similar one.
2. Ask the learner a series of related positional computation questions such as the following. What do you get when you add the number *in* the box to the number *above* the box? What is the total when you add the numbers on *top* and to the *left* of the box? What is the difference between the number *below* the box and the number to the *right* of it?
3. The learner should point to or touch each number as it is noted.
4. Use and discuss a variety of positional terms such as "in," "within," "on top," "above," "over," "under," "below," "underneath," and so forth.

AN EASIER VARIATION:

1. Have the learner identify single numbers according to the stated location. If asked, for example, about the numeral *above* or *on top of* the square she should respond four.
2. The learner might also show the "how manyness" of the identified number by using objects. For example, if asked about the number to the *right* of the square she should say three and place 3 objects beside it.

■ AN ADVANCED VARIATION:

1. Have the learners mentally compute and answer questions relating to three (or more) locations. For example, if asked to add the numbers on *top* of, to the *right* of, and *in* the square, the mental math required is 4 + 3 + 2 = 9.
2. As further *challenges,* any or all of the following variations might be attempted: (a) Use a mix of operations such as add the first two numbers and subtract a third; (b) Include larger numbers such as 8, 9, 12, 15; (c) Call for the computation of 4 or 5 or more numbers. Do so by placing numerals at the corners of a square or using shapes such as hexagons and octagons.

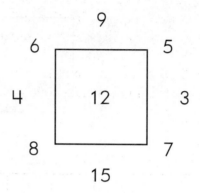

Before/After Roll

■ WHY DO IT?

To practice number order 1 through 13
To practice addition to 12

■ HERE'S HOW!

1. Use two 1 through 6 dice, a number line from 1 through 13 and a marker for each player (a button, bean, small rock, or bottle cap).
2. Each player, in turn, rolls the dice and adds the numbers together. She then puts a marker on the number line, either one number before or one number after the number total shown on the dice.
3. If both the before and after numbers are covered, the player must pass.
4. When the entire number line is covered the player with the most markers on it wins.

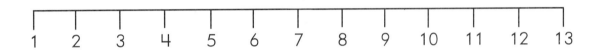

■ AN EASIER VARIATION:

1. Provide a 1 through 6 dot die, a 0 through 7 number line, and a marker for each learner.
2. Have the learner roll the die and count the dots. The learner might like to pretend that the marker is a frog or a rabbit as he jumps it from the first number on the line to the number rolled.
3. Then ask the learner to jump the marker to the number *before* or *after* the number rolled and to identify that number. The learner should state, "_____ is the number before _____," *or* "_____ is the number after _____."

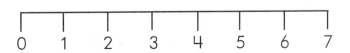

ADVANCED VARIATION:

1. Use three 1 through 6 dice, a number line to 20, and a marker for each player (buttons or beans).
2. Have each player, in turn, roll the dice and mentally add the three numbers together.
3. The player must then put a marker on the number line either two numbers *before* or two numbers *after* the dice number total. She must also explain why the marker was placed in that specific location.
4. If both the *before* and *after* numbers are already covered the player must pass.
5. When the entire number line is covered, the player with the most markers on it wins.

Drop the Money

WHY DO IT?

To practice counting by fives

To practice addition and subtraction skills when using money

HERE'S HOW!

1. Provide five pennies and five nickels for each player.
2. Obtain a shoe box lid for each player. Color half of the lid with a red marker or crayon.
3. The player takes all of the coins in hand, shakes them, and drops them into the lid.
4. The player finds *only* the value of the coins that fall into the *red side* of the lid. (*Note:* The player should be taught to count the nickels first by 5's and then add the pennies by 1's.)

AN EASIER VARIATION:

Play the above activity with pennies only; use ten pennies initially, then increase to fifteen pennies, and then twenty pennies.

AN ADVANCED VARIATION:

Play the original activity with five dimes and five quarters in addition to the pennies and nickels.

ANOTHER ADVANCED VARIATION:

1. Play the original activity and have the player find the value of the money on both sides of the lid.
2. Then have the player determine which side of the lid has the most money.
3. If she is able, have the player figure out how much more money is on one side of the lid than on the other by using subtraction.

Coin Trade

WHY DO IT?

To practice values with pennies, nickels, dimes, and quarters

To practice addition skills

     =

HERE'S HOW!

1. Provide penny, nickel, dime, and quarter Money Grids for learners to work with. (Real coins taped to some of the respective Money Grids might further aid in understanding.)
2. Have the learners show and tell how many penny grids it takes to equal a nickel, a dime, a quarter.
3. As a *challenge,* learners might also practice placing the smaller Money Grids on the larger ones to match and count values. For example, if 35 cents is called for it might be matched with a 25 cent (quarter) grid and a 10 cent (dime) grid, but it could also be matched in other ways such as with three 10 cent (dime) grids and a 5 cent (nickel) grid.

AN EASY VARIATION:

1. Put one penny, nickel, dime, and quarter in a small paper bag.
2. Assemble a spinner that has the words and pictures of a penny, a nickel, a dime, and a quarter in designated sections (see the illustration and Appendix A for directions on making spinners).
3. Take turns spinning the spinner and have the learners note which coin is called for. Then have a learner put his or her hand in the bag, without looking, and try to feel and pull out the coin that the spinner showed. Replace the coin for the next learner's turn.

4. If scorekeeping is desired, allow 1 point for each correct grab. The first player to get five points, or any agreed upon total, wins.

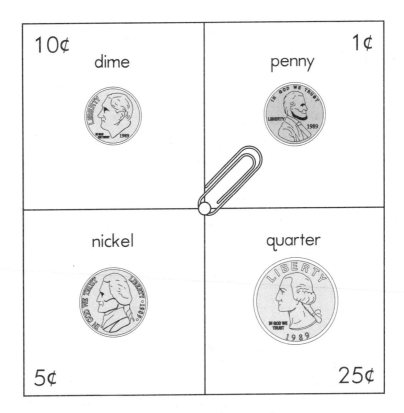

(Hold the paper clip in place with a pencil
point and spin with your other hand.)

■ AN ADVANCED VARIATION:

1. Collect five pennies, five nickels, five dimes, and five quarters.
2. Talk about how much each coin is worth. Have the learners use the Money Grids to explain the value of each coin
3. Put a coin on the table as the *target* amount. Have the learners use the other coins to add up to the *target* value. For example, if a dime is the *target,* the learners might show equivalent value with two nickels, or one nickel and five pennies, or ten pennies.
4. Put out two coins as the *target* amount and repeat the process. Continue by having the learners find equivalent values for three, four, or five coins, so long as they remain interested and successful.

(*Note:* You may wish to make multiple copies of the penny, nickel, and dime grids on the next page. It may be helpful to glue the nickel, dime, and quarter coin copies on back of the matching Money Grids.)

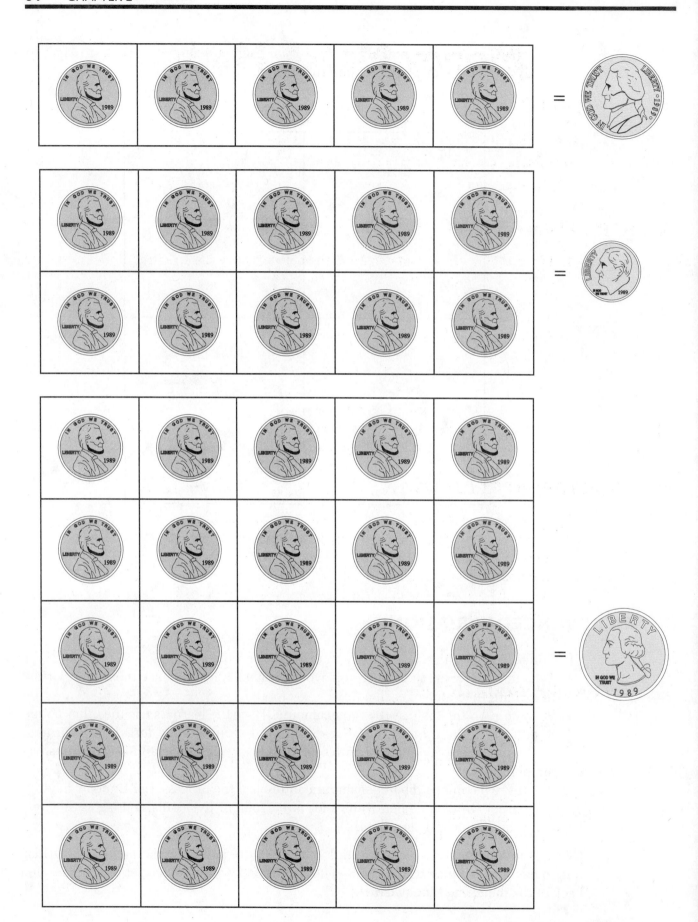

Money Match Math

▓ WHY DO IT?

To practice identifying and learning the value of different coins

To practice coin value exchanges (5 pennies = a nickel, 10 pennies = a dime).

To gain experience with different coin combinations that have the same value

▓ HERE'S HOW!

1. When playing *Money Match Math* the object is to earn a specific amount of money such as 20 cents or 50 cents.
2. To do so each player takes a turn rolling a die and acquires the number of pennies equal to the number shown on the die.
3. As each player acquires enough pennies, they can be traded for other coins; for example 5 pennies should be traded for a nickel, and two nickels (or one nickel and five pennies) for a dime, and so forth. (*Note:* If learners find the trading of coins difficult, use the Money Grids from the *Coin Trade* activity.)
4. The first player to reach the stated amount wins the game.
5. As a further *challenge,* ask each player to figure out how many different coin combinations equal the specified amount.

▓ AN ALTERNATE VARIATION:

1. Read the book *26 Letters and 99 Cents,*[1] by Tana Hoban.
2. Using the 99 cent section of the book and a variety of real coins, ask the learner to identify those used in the illustrations; he should also place an actual coin, or set of coins, on each illustration to match those pictured.
3. When the learner has completed the money matching for an illustration, help him to determine the total value.
4. A discussion of other coin combinations that will yield the same value is also advised.

▓ AN EASIER VARIATION:

1. Make task cards that have a line drawn down the middle to create two equal sections.
2. Use cellophane tape to fasten a coin (penny, nickel, dime, or quarter) to one section of each card.
3. Provide a variety of loose coins and ask the learner to select and place a matching coin on the other section of each task card. (*Note:* Be sure to have the learner closely examine both sides of each coin; otherwise she will sometimes insist that a penny is only a penny when the face side is showing. Also carefully examine shiny new coins versus older ones that are worn and dull.)
4. Teach the learner the name of each coin.

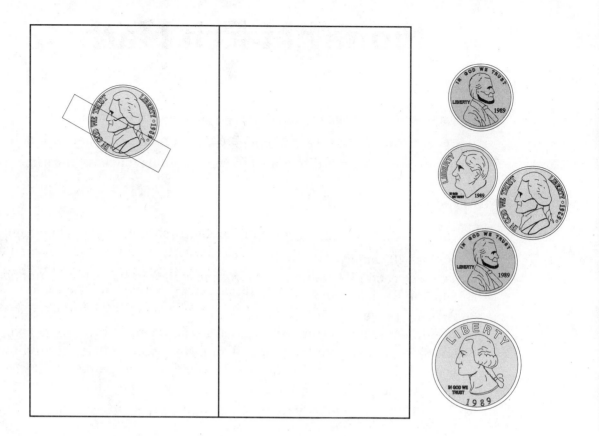

![] AN ADVANCED VARIATION:

1. Provide the learner with a selection of things he might like to buy, such as items from a children's restaurant menu or selections from a toy catalog.
2. Ask him to pick an item, find the price, and show the coins needed to purchase it.
3. As a further *challenge,* the activity might be reversed by writing the prices for various items in terms of quarters, dimes, nickels, and pennies and asking the child to figure the total price of that item. (A peanut butter and jelly sandwich, for example, might cost 3 quarters + 1 dime + 1 nickel + 3 pennies.)

What Price?

■ ## WHY DO IT?

> To simulate real life problem-solving experiences
> To enhance addition and subtraction skills

HERE'S HOW!

1. Help the learners set up a small "pretend" store using pictures from magazines, newspaper grocery ads, empty labeled cans and boxes, and so forth. (The pictures may be pasted on cards.) Write a price on each, but keep the numbers low.
2. Have the learner select two items and add the numbers together to see how much she owes. As the learners become more proficient in addition, increase the number of items to be bought.

AN EASIER VARIATION:

1. Have the learners select two items and indicate which one costs the most (the larger number).
2. If the activity is to be played with more than one learner, ask the learners to each select an item and determine who owes the most and the least.
3. Have the learner place the priced items in numerical order from least to most expensive.

AN ADVANCED VARIATION:

1. Have the learner locate favorite items for sale in newspaper advertisements, toy catalogs, and so forth. He should select two items and determine the total cost.
2. If ready, the learner might also determine the total for 3 or 4 or more items.
3. As a *challenge,* the learner might also use subtraction to determine how much more expensive one item is than another.

A MORE ADVANCED VARIATION:

1. Read the story, *Alexander Who Used to Be Rich Last Sunday,*[2] by Judith Viorst.
2. Provide a piece of paper with 100 cents written on it (ignore the dollar sign and decimal at first).
3. Ask the learners to subtract the amounts Alexander spent. Share the findings and discuss what each means.

4. A *challenge* might involve having Alexander receive additional money from time to time, such as 50 cents for sweeping the sidewalk.
5. A *further challenge* might be to have the learners help make up a story about a person who has a certain sum of money, and who wants to buy some items. Have the learners repeatedly subtract the cost of the items to see whether the person has enough money.

Number Mystery Puzzle

■ WHY DO IT?

To instill a curiosity for number *puzzles*

To practice mental math computation

To achieve *answers* by manipulating numbers in a variety of sequences

■ HERE'S HOW!

1. Write the numbers 1 through 9 on small circles of paper.
2. Photocopy the Number Mystery Grids.
3. Have the learner select a *sum* (such as 8) that she will try to obtain.
4. Then ask the learner to place number circles on the puzzle spots so they will equal the desired sum in each direction (see solution for sum 8).
5. Challenge the learner to discover as many different puzzle solutions as possible.

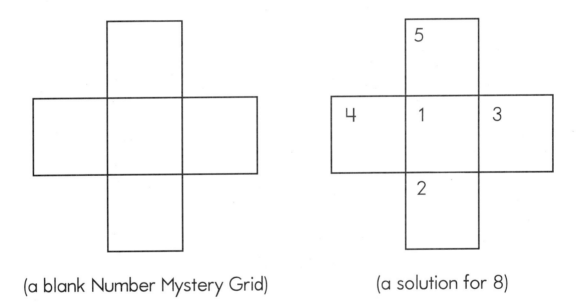

(a blank Number Mystery Grid)   (a solution for 8)

■ AN EASIER VARIATION:

1. The learner will need *Number Mystery Grids*, circles cut from paper with the numbers 1 through 9 written on them, and small objects (beans, pebbles, or pennies) to assist in the solution of the puzzles.
2. Provide the learner with a Number Mystery Puzzle that has been solved and ask that he *prove* whether or not the solution is correct.

3. To *prove* (or *disprove*) the solution, the learner must first count out objects equal to each numeral and place them in the grid spaces beside each of the number circles. (See example for sum 8.)

4. Next have the learner count all of the objects along one line (horizontal) and then the other (vertical) to find whether the sums are the same.

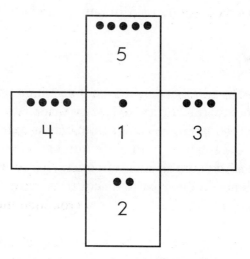

■ AN ADVANCED VARIATION:

1. Provide two sets of number circles 1 through 9 and a 3 × 3 *Number Mystery Puzzle*.

2. Ask the learner to place number circles on the puzzle spots so that they will equal the same sum in all directions (see a solution for sum 15).

3. Challenge the learner to discover as many different puzzle solutions as possible.

2	7	6
9	5	1
4	3	8

Calculator Shopping

■ WHY DO IT?

To practice using a calculator

To see how estimation can be helpful

To practice basic facts

■ HERE'S HOW!

1. Show the learners how to enter numbers, the addition sign, and the equal sign on a calculator. (*Note:* Exercise care when entering numbers since no visual record of errors will be available.) Then take the learners and a calculator to the store or go catalog shopping.

2. As each item is selected, talk about the price rounded to the nearest dollar. Explain that the rounded number is not the exact cost of the item, but that it is a close estimation. He should enter the rounded numbers and keep a running total on the calculator.

3. When finished at the checkout stand, check to see how close the calculator total, using rounded numbers, is to the exact total. If the calculator rounded total is a little low (or high) how might this be adjusted for on the next shopping trip?

▨ AN EASIER VARIATION:

1. Have the learners use the calculator to count. To do so enter **1** and **+**.
2. Then ask the child to press the equals button one time and say the number displayed, press the equals button a second time and say that number, a third time, and so forth. The calculator will display **1, 2, 3,** and so forth. (*Note:* This will work with nearly all basic calculators, but do try it in advance to be certain.)
3. The learners might also try skip counting (counting by multiples) in the same manner. For example, to count by 2s enter **2** and **+** and the equals button. The calculator will then display **2, 4, 6,** and so forth. Have the learners predict which number will come next. Is there a pattern? If done for 3s the calculator will display **3, 6, 9,** and so forth. (*Note:* Activities such as this help to provide *groundwork* for learning multiplication facts.)

▨ ADVANCED VARIATIONS:

1. Use a calculator rather than flash cards when practicing basic facts. When doing so one player might call out a basic fact such as 7 plus 8 and enter it into the calculator. As soon as the other player has answered she should press the equals button to find out whether the answer given was correct.
2. For students needing a *challenge,* higher-level thinking and basic fact practice can be provided simultaneously. For example, practice with multiplying by 6s, without telling the learner that is what she is doing, can be set up by secretly pressing the 6 and × buttons and then handing it to the student. By trial and error she might record × 3 = 18, × 6 = 36, × 2 = 12, × 4 = 24.

   By this time she will likely have discovered that multiplication by 6 is what is taking place. (*Note:* The calculator being used must utilize a constant feature; to determine if this is the case simply try the above example.)

Undercover Adder

WHY DO IT?

To practice addition or subtraction facts

HERE'S HOW!

1. Find covers such as bottle caps, buttons, or cut out small pieces of paper for each of the numbers on the *Undercover Adder Game Board*.
2. Place a cover over each number on the game board so that the numbers cannot be seen.
3. The first player uncovers two numbers and adds them together. If correct he keeps the covers. If incorrect, the covers are returned to the board.
4. The second player continues the game in the same way. The player with the most covers at the end of the game wins.
5. Learners who find the addition game fairly easy might play the game using subtraction. (*Note:* The players need to understand that the smaller number must be subtracted from the larger.)

AN EASIER VARIATION:

1. Make a Counter board with only the numbers 0 through 5. Place bottle caps, open side up, on any two numbers. Then count the number of beans into each cap to correspond to the covered numbers. Combine the beans from the two caps and count them to solve the addition problem.

0	4	3	2	0	1	3
3	2	5	1	3	5	5
5	1	2	3	5	2	4

(A Counter Board for 0 - 5)

2. The beans might also be used for comparative subtraction. If, for example, 4 and 3 are the number of beans being considered, the 4 beans should be placed in a line parallel to the 3 beans (as shown below). The learners might then say that 4 is 1 more than 3.

■ ADVANCED VARIATIONS:

1. A more complex activity results when learners are asked to uncover and add three or more numbers.
2. Keep a running total of each player's score and the highest score wins.
3. If an older learner is practicing her multiplication facts, have her multiply instead of add.

UNDERCOVER ADDER BOARD

0	4	3	2	0	1	3
4	7	2	5	<u>6</u>	3	2
<u>6</u>	8	1	7	4	<u>9</u>	<u>6</u>
7	<u>9</u>	4	<u>6</u>	8	2	7
3	2	5	1	3	5	5
4	7	2	5	<u>6</u>	3	2
<u>6</u>	0	1	7	4	<u>9</u>	<u>4</u>
5	8	3	7	<u>9</u>	8	<u>6</u>

Math Tic-Tac-Toe

■ WHY DO IT?

To practice addition or subtraction facts

■ HERE'S HOW!

1. Make a *Tic-Tac-Toe* board with addition or subtraction problems in each space (see illustration).
2. Find markers such as beans and rocks for each player.
3. Play *Tic-Tac-Toe* as usual except players must answer the problem in the square correctly before they can put a marker on the space.

3 + 4	6 – 2	2 + 5
9 – 8	4 + 4	7 – 3
6 + 4	8 – 2	5 + 4

■ AN EASIER VARIATION:

1. Make a *Tic-Tac-Toe* board that has a small number of dots in each section. (*Note:* For this variation the learner needs to count and say the corresponding numbers but does not need to add or subtract.)
2. Play *Tic-Tac-Toe* as usual except that each player must count the dots and say the number for the desired square before being allowed to place his marker.
3. If a further *challenge* is desired, play another game where the learner must say the number that is one less than the number in the desired square. (If it is necessary to assist the learner, cover up one of the dots in the square and count the dots now showing.)

■ AN ADVANCED VARIATION:

1. Play a *Tic-Tac-Toe* game that involves a larger grid and both addition and subtraction problems. (*Note:* Each player should be expected to use the correct operation without being told.)
2. As a *further challenge,* include problems in each space that have a series of three numbers and involve two operations such as 3 + 6 – 2 = ?

Plus and Minus

■ WHY DO IT?

To practice addition and subtraction

To develop logical thinking skills

To encourage estimation and mental math

■ HERE'S HOW!

1. Make one set of large cards numbered 2 through 15. Also photocopy and cut apart sets of small number cards and the plus and minus cards for each player.
2. Place a set of small number cards face up in front of each player.
3. Place the large number cards face down between the players.
4. The players, in turn, each draw a large number card. Each player then must use two of his or her small number cards together with either the addition or subtraction symbol to equal the large number card. The plus and minus cards may be reused as many times as needed in the game.
5. The first player to use up all (or most of) her or his small number cards wins.

1	2	3	4	5	6
7	8	9	10	+	−

(Small Number Cards)

■ AN EASIER VARIATION:

1. Make one set of large number cards with the numbers 2 through 10 on them. Also provide each player with a paper that has a line drawn across the middle to create a top half and a bottom half.

2. Obtain markers of two different colors, such as green and red M&Ms®. (During play the green M&Ms will only be placed on the top half of the paper and the red will only be placed on the bottom half of the paper.)

3. The large number cards are to be placed face down in the middle of the table with the top card turned up.

4. Every player is then to place an M&M total on his or her piece of paper that equals the value of the turned over card. For example, if the turned over card was six, each player would place a total of six M&Ms on his or her piece of paper. One player might have 3 green M&Ms on the top half of the paper and 3 red on the bottom half of the paper. Another player might have 1 green M&M on the top half of the paper and 5 red ones on the bottom half of the paper.

5. Each player must also say the number sentence that matches his or her M&M arrangement. For example, one player, in the above example, would say "3 + 3 = 6". The other player would say "1 + 5 = 6".

6. Also take time to show and talk about other groupings (as 4 + 2 = 6. 6 + 0 = 6, etc.) that might be made.

7. After each round the players may be allowed to eat their M&Ms!

■ AN ADVANCED VARIATION:

Play the original game but make the following adjustments.

1. Make small number cards numbered from 1 to 20 for each player.

2. The players may use two or three number cards in a number sentence to equal the large number card that is turned over. For example, if the large number card is a 12, the player might use the small number cards 10, 8, and 6 in the sentence 10 + 8 − 6 = 12.

Add It Up

■ WHY DO IT?

To practice addition facts to ten

■ HERE'S HOW!

1. Photocopy and cut apart the cards below or make a set from index cards. Shuffle and deal them all out to the players.
2. The first player shows one card to the other players. All players try to write down as many addition problems as possible that equal the number on the card. (*Note:* Some players will find it helpful to use objects such as beans or paper clips to help figure out workable number combinations. For example, 6 might be shown as ••• ••• 3 + 3, or as •••• •• 4 + 2.)
3. The players take turns showing their cards. Each addition problem is worth one point. If winning is desirable, the player with the most points wins.

| 1 | 2 | 3 | 4 | 5 |
| 6 | 7 | 8 | 9 | 10 |

■ AN ALTERNATE VARIATION:

1. Use the cards numbered 2 through 10 from a regular deck of playing cards. Mix them and deal five (or more) cards to each player.
2. If, when examining the cards dealt, the players find that two of their cards add to the value of a third, they may lay those cards down immediately. For example, if a player has a 2, a 3, and a 5, she should state that 2 plus 3 equals 5 and show them face up.
3. The first player then looks at her remaining cards and decides which of the following questions to ask (one question only): (a) If the player holds two cards with small numbers that add up to ten or less, she might ask, "Do you have a _____ (the sum of the two cards)?" If, for example the player has a 3 and a 4, she should ask for a 7.

(b) If, however, a card with a large number is held, she should ask for two cards with small numbers that will add up to that sum. For example, if the player has a 9, she might ask for a 6 and a 3 (**or** any combination that adds up to nine).

4. If player one receives the called for card(s) she may play them and continue asking. However, if player two does not have the card(s) asked for, player one must draw a card from the pile. If successful, player one may continue asking, but if not her turn is finished.
5. Player two then begins his turn.
6. The first person to get rid of all of his or her cards wins.

AN EASIER VARIATION:

1. Make cards with numerals and matching numbers of dots. Have children match beans or buttons to the dots.

 etc.

2. Add a second card and repeat the process. Add the numbers together and find the answer by counting the total number of beans or buttons.

MORE DIFFICULT VARIATIONS:

1. Make a deck of cards from 1 through 20 (or higher). Use two or three cards at a turn to *Add It Up*.
2. Play *Take Away Subtraction* by drawing two cards and having the learner take away the smaller amount from the larger. Initially this should be done with objects. For example if 9 and 4 are the numbers being considered, the learner should place 9 beans in a row and then take away 4 to show 5 remaining. This could be recorded as $9 - 4 = 5$.
3. Also play *Comparative Subtraction* where nothing is taken away, but rather the amounts are compared. For the cards 9 and 4, the 9 beans might be placed in a line and 4 beans in another parallel line (as shown). Then compare and consider, how many more beans will it take to make 9?

Do This

■ **WHY DO IT?**

To enhance number recognition and computation skills
To physically act out math fact solutions to ten or more

2	4	5	3
5	1	4	6
2	6	1	5
4	2	5	3

■ **HERE'S HOW!**

1. Help the learners to draw a large square, circle, or triangle on a piece of butcher paper (or with chalk on a sidewalk). Divide the figure into sections and randomly number each from 1 through 6.
2. Choose an activity (or have several to select from) such as clapping, jumping, walking on tip toes, patting your head, touching toes, or blinking that can be acted out easily.
3. At a player's turn he throws two bean bags onto two different numbers of the figure.
4. The player must then identify the two numbers, add them together, and act out the answer. If, for example, the bean bags land on a 5 and a 3, the student might clap 8 times. (*Note:* If the learner is unsure, allow him to place 5 objects on that space and 3 on the other and then physically count out 5, 6, 7, 8.)

■ AN EASIER VARIATION:

1. Draw a large square, circle, or triangle on a piece of butcher paper (or with chalk on a sidewalk), divide it into sections, and randomly number each from 1 through 9.
2. Choose an activity that can be easily acted out such as clapping, jumping, or touching toes.
3. At a player's turn he will throw just one bean bag onto the figure.
4. The player must then identify the number landed on and act out the answer. If, for example, the bean bag lands on a 7, the player might jump 7 times. (*Note:* If the learner is unsure, help her to place the correct number of objects on that space and then physically count them.)

■ AN ADVANCED VARIATION:

1. To play *Subtract from 10,* draw a large figure on a piece of butcher paper (or with chalk on a sidewalk), divide it into sections, and randomly number each from 1 through 6. Also select an activity that can be easily acted out such as clapping, jumping, or touching toes.
2. At his or her turn each player will throw a bean bag onto the figure.
3. The player must then identify the number landed on, mentally subtract that number from 10, verbally state the equation, and act out the answer. If, for example, the bean bag lands on a 4 and touching toes is the designated activity, he must then say 10 minus 4 equals 6, and then touch his toes 6 times.

Milk Carton Calculators

■ WHY DO IT?

To practice basic addition and subtraction facts

To help students make connections between visual representations and written numbers

■ HERE'S HOW!

1. Make a milk carton calculator and a series of problem and answer cards (see directions for both).
2. When using the milk carton calculator the learner looks at the addition (or subtraction) problem side of the card and says what he thinks the answer is.
3. She then checks the answer by sliding the card (problem side up) into the top slot of the milk carton calculator.
4. When the card slides out through the bottom slot, the correct answer to the problem will be shown.

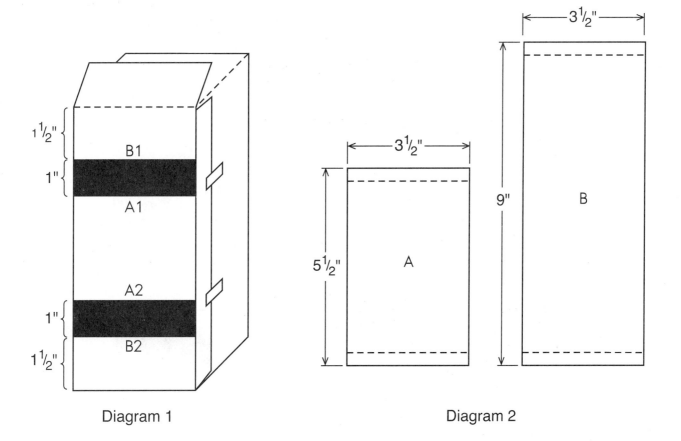

Diagram 1   Diagram 2

■ CONSTRUCTING A MILK CARTON CALCULATOR:

- Sterilize a half gallon milk carton.
- Cut each of the four corners of the top portion of the carton.
- Cut a 1 inch wide by 3¼ inch long slot that is 1½ inches from the top of the carton and a second slot with the same dimensions that is 1½ inches from the bottom of the carton (Diagram 1).
- Using card stock, cut out one rectangle with the dimensions 3½ inches by 5½ inches and label it **A** and cut a second rectangle with the dimensions 3½ inches by 9 inches and label it **B**.
- On each of the shorter ends of the rectangles, fold the ends over ½ inch from the end (Diagram 2).
- Place rectangle **A** inside the milk carton, bringing the folded ends to the outside of the carton, through the cut out sections. The top flap will come through the top opening, and the bottom flap will come through the bottom opening.
- Using masking tape, attach the flaps on the front of the carton (Diagram 3).
- Place rectangle **B** inside the milk carton bringing the folded ends to the outside of the carton, through the cut out sections. The top flap will come through the top opening, and the bottom flap will come through the bottom opening.
- Tape with masking tape. Reinforce edges with tape to handle abuse and tape top flaps flat.
- You may wish to cover the entire container with decorative contact paper. If so, use scissors or a utility knife to cut out the slots.

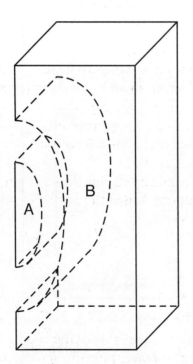
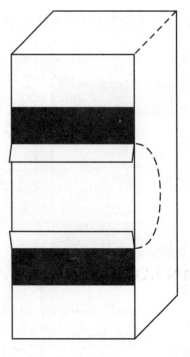

Diagram 3

▮ CONSTRUCTING PROBLEM AND ANSWER CARDS:

- Obtain index or other cards that are at least 2 inches by 3¼ inches.
- On the problem side of the card write an addition or subtraction fact question (or other appropriate problem). On the other side, write the answer to the problem. (*Note:* the card must be flipped over from top to bottom and then the answer written so that the it will show proper side up.)

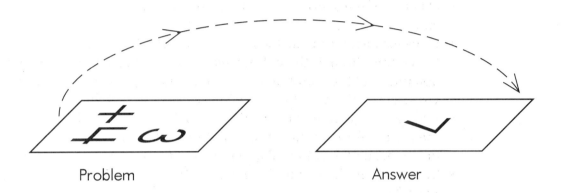

Problem   Answer

(Flip card over end for end)

▮ AN EASIER VARIATION:

1. Assemble a milk carton calculator using the directions shown.
2. Make problem and answer cards from small index cards (or other card stock at least 2 inches by 3¼ inches). On one side of the card draw a number of objects (such as five stars) and on the other side write the corresponding number 5.
3. The learner must then count the number of objects on the problem side of the card and say what she thinks the number is.
3. The learner's answer is then checked by sliding the card (problem side up) into the top slot of the milk carton calculator. When the card slides out through the bottom slot, the actual number will show.

▮ AN ADVANCED VARIATION:

1. Perform the original activity, but write three addend addition and/or subtraction problems such as 2 + 5 − 4 = on the front side of the card.
2. For students needing a further *challenge,* play the activity using simple multiplication or division problems and/or word problems.

Five Fact Flower

■ WHY DO IT?

To practice basic addition and subtraction facts

To increase awareness of the "how manyness" of numbers

To practice basic multiplication and division facts

■ HERE'S HOW!

1. Each learner draws or is given a flower that has a center space and five petals.
2. A number, such as 8, is placed in the center space.
3. The learner tries to think of five different math equations (addition or subtraction) that equal the center space number. He writes one equation in each petal of the flower.
4. If competition is desired, learners might be placed in pairs. The learner who finishes filling in all five petals first wins a point, but only if all five equations are correct. If any of the five equations are incorrect, the other learner automatically receives the point.

AN EASIER VARIATION:

1. Give the learner a large drawn flower that has a center spot and five petals on it.
2. A number, such as 5, is placed in the center space.
3. Provide a variety of different small objects such as bug counters, pebbles, or sunflower seeds to place on the petals.
4. The learner must then place an equal amount of objects in each petal so that each matches the center space number.

AN ADVANCED VARIATION:

1. Play the original game and allow any correct addition, subtraction, multiplication, or division equations to fill the petals.
2. Restrictions, such as limiting the use of zero and/or one, may sometimes be advisable.

Addition Partners

■ WHY DO IT?

To practice addition with missing addends

■ HERE'S HOW!

1. Provide an *Addition Partners Sheet* and a die marked with 1, 1, 2, 2, 3, and 3.
2. The player then rolls the die and writes that number in the first square.

$$\boxed{3} \;+\; \boxed{} \;=\; \boxed{7}$$

3. Then ask the player to figure out what number goes in the second square to make the number sentence correct. (Counting manipulatives such as beans, buttons, or small stones may help the learner figure out the problems.)

■ AN EASIER VARIATION:

1. Provide a large sheet of paper with a single row of three large boxes similar to those in the *Addition Partners Sheet*. Write in the symbols + and = but don't dwell on them. If the learner asks what they are, explain in simple terms. Also use a die marked •, •, ••, ••, •••, and •••.
2. Gather a supply of simple objects (beans, paper clips, or blocks) to use as counters.
3. Place a number of objects (perhaps •••••) in the *answer* box.
4. Have the player roll the die and place the corresponding number of counters in the first box (perhaps ••).
5. Then ask how many counters must go in the second box so there will be the same number of counters in boxes 1 and 2 together as there are in box 3? (Allow the learner to place and count manipulatives as she works toward a solution.)

$$\boxed{\bullet\bullet} \;+\; \boxed{} \;=\; \boxed{\begin{smallmatrix}\bullet\;\;\bullet\\\bullet\\\bullet\;\;\bullet\end{smallmatrix}}$$

ADDITION PARTNERS SHEET

$$\square + \square = \boxed{7}$$

$$\square + \square = \boxed{5}$$

$$\square + \square = \boxed{8}$$

$$\square + \square = \boxed{4}$$

$$\square + \square = \boxed{6}$$

$$\square + \square = \boxed{9}$$

$$\square + \square = \boxed{3}$$

$$\square + \square = \boxed{10}$$

$$\square + \square = \boxed{12}$$

◼ AN ADVANCED VARIATION:

1. Develop an *Addition Partners Sheet* with 3 addends plus an answer box (see sample).
2. Let the learner randomly place numbers 12 to 18 (or larger) in the answer column.
3. The learner then rolls two dice (numbered 1 through 6), places those numbers in two of the addend squares, and then solves for the third square. (It is possible the third square could be zero.)

$$\square + \square + \square = \boxed{17}$$

Works Cited

1. Tana Hoban, *26 Letters and 99 Cents* (New York: Greenwillow Books Division of William Morrow and Company, 1988).
2. Judith Viorst, *Alexander, Who Used to Be Rich Last Sunday* (New York: Atheneum, 1979).

CHAPTER 3

Measurement

Measurement is one of the most important mathematical skills needed in daily life. The best way for children to develop such skills is by allowing them numerous hands-on experiences. They need experiences with: (1) making comparisons (heavier and lighter, longer or shorter); (2) ordering several objects (which holds the least to the most); (3) measuring with everyday items (the table is 7 hand lengths long); and (4) measuring with standard units for distance, capacity, temperature, and time.

To gain an understanding of needed measurement concepts young learners need to repeat such activities in numerous and varied ways. This is especially important in light of the fact that most young learners will not yet have achieved measurement *conservation* concepts. A young child, for example, who has not yet developed an understanding of *conservation of length,* when shown two identical pencils side by side will say that they measure the same length, but when the position of the pencils is changed he or she will likely insist that the pencil measurements are now different. Thus, it is important that young learners have many such experiences and also be exposed to measurement tasks that relate to *conservation of volume, conservation of area,* and *conservation of weight.* Finally, it is important to realize that no amount of telling or showing will teach a child such concepts of conservation; his or her learning will, instead, result from many varied personal experiences

The activities provided in this chapter help young children to deal effectively with a wide range of important measurement skills and concepts. An added bonus is that these experiences can set the stage for important mathematical conversations between parents and children and between teachers and children.

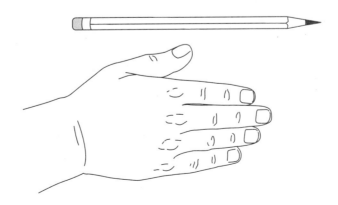

111

Line Up

■ WHY DO IT?

To observe and manipulate objects making comparisons using such words as "shortest" and "tallest"

■ HERE'S HOW!

Have the learner rearrange items around the house (or the school room) from shortest to tallest. Use books, people, tools, stuffed animals, drinking glasses, and so forth.

■ AN EASIER VARIATION:

1. Cut straws or strips of cardboard into different lengths. Encourage the learners to use a common base as they lay them in order from shortest to longest or longest to shortest.
2. The learner might also compare the straws when they are in upright positions. To do so stick them in play dough or clay and discuss which is tallest and which is shortest.

■ ANOTHER EASIER VARIATION:

1. Roll play dough into different sized balls and have the learner determine which is smallest and which is largest.

2. Roll the play dough into snakes and have the learner compare longest and shortest lengths.
3. Discuss and use related terms such as "biggest," "fattest," "thinnest," and so forth.

AN ADVANCED VARIATION:

1. Discuss how the heights of objects that cannot be moved might be compared. How might we find out whether the flagpole at the school or the one at city hall is the tallest, or which of two trees several miles apart is shorter.
2. Guide the learners to note how the shadows objects cast may be used to approximate their heights.
3. Finally, if the learners are ready for a *challenge,* find out how surveyors use triangles (and precise instruments) to determine such measurements.

Stick Walk

■ WHY DO IT?

To gain experience making length comparisons

To practice using math vocabulary (such as shorter and longer).

■ HERE'S HOW!

1. Go for a short walk outside and have the learners collect five to ten sticks.
2. Ask the learners to arrange the sticks in order from longest to shortest. Mix them up and now have them arrange the sticks from shortest to longest. Ask the learners to indicate the shortest and the longest.
3. Randomly select two or three of the sticks. Ask the learners to indicate which of the sticks in this *new* set is shortest and which is longest?

■ AN EASIER VARIATION:

1. Photocopy and cut paper rods, as shown on the following pages into strips. Ask the learner to match them to the appropriate spaces in the rod tray. Have the learner notice the differences in length and point out the shortest and longest rods. (*Note:* In order for young learners to handle them more easily, the paper rods might be pasted on tagboard or heavy paper.)
2. As a slightly more difficult task, have the learner arrange the paper rods from shortest to longest without using the rod tray.

■ AN ADVANCED VARIATION:

1. Ask the learners to color the sectioned paper rods as units with two different alternating colors (as yellow and green). Cut out the rods and ask the learners to put them in order from shortest to longest.

(Examples: a colored rod for **6** and a rod for **3**)

Rods for 1 to 10

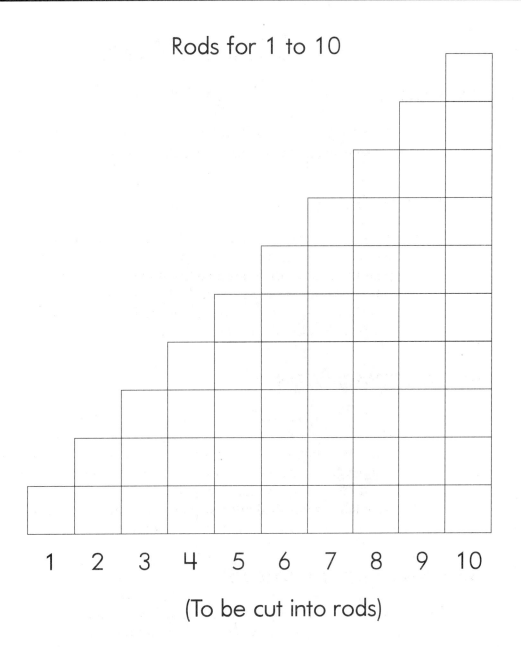

1 2 3 4 5 6 7 8 9 10

(To be cut into rods)

2. Ask the learners to count the sections in the shortest rod, the next larger rod, the longest rod. Then randomly select two rods and ask the learners to indicate the shortest and longest. Have the learners count the number of sections in the shortest rod and those in the longest rod. Ask the learners how many more sections the longer rod has than the shorter one?

3. Select a different pair of rods and have the learners tell how much larger (or smaller) one is. Have the learners explain how they figured it out.

Rod Tray

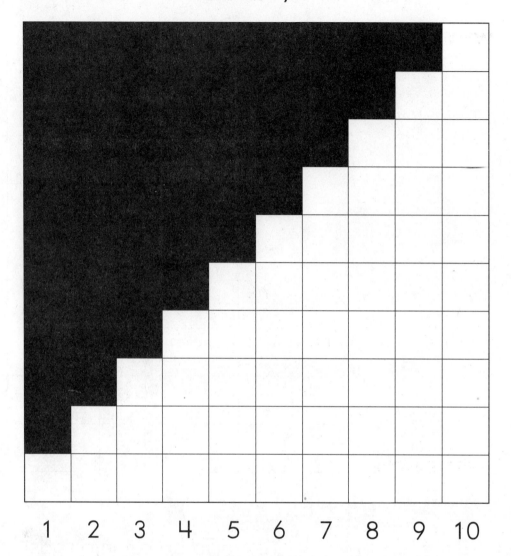

1   2   3   4   5   6   7   8   9   10

Rock and Roll Measure

■ WHY DO IT?

To make comparisons between lengths using the words "closer," "farther," and/or similar vocabulary

■ HERE'S HOW!

1. Provide a target (such as a small can, a bean, or a bottle cap), paper strips for measuring, and one small round rock per player.
2. The target is placed in the middle of the floor and each player rolls his or her rock toward the marker, trying to get as close as possible.
3. Players compare how far their rocks are from the target by marking the distances on strips of paper and laying the strips next to each other. The players must then use the words "closer" and "farther" when talking about the position of their rocks.
4. If the players choose to keep score, flip a coin after each round. If heads turns up, the player *closest* to the marker wins a point. If tails, the *farthest* player from the marker wins a point. The first player to get five points wins.

■ AN EASIER VARIATION:

1. Cut several lengths of string and place them in a box.
2. Have the learner choose two strings and compare their lengths by laying the strings next to each other. Which string is shorter? Which is longer?
3. Replace the strings and try again.

■ AN ADVANCED VARIATION:

1. Use standard measurements when playing the original Rock and Roll Measure activity. Use a ruler (see Appendix A) to measure the distances and find who is closest to the nearest inch (or centimeter).

2. If the learner wants a greater *challenge*, he might be asked to determine how much closer one player is than another.

People Compare

■ WHY DO IT?

To observe size comparisons and use the words "taller" and "shorter" and/or similar measurement vocabulary

■ HERE'S HOW!

1. Instruct the learners to have each person in their families compare his or her height to the following objects: chair, refrigerator, or lamp. Record the comparisons by writing the peoples' names on a chart like the one shown. For example, when compared to the refrigerator, brother Jason might be shorter, Mom about the same height, and Dad taller.
2. Have the learners draw a picture of their family members from tallest to shortest.
3. The learners should find something taller than any of their family members. Find something shorter. Draw a picture showing these comparisons.

	SHORTER	ABOUT THE SAME	TALLER
CHAIR			
REFRIGERATOR			
LAMP			

■ AN EASIER VARIATION:

Stand two family members together and compare their heights. Who is taller? Shorter? Stand by another person. Now who is shorter? Taller? The learner may be shorter than one family member but taller than another.

ANOTHER EASIER VARIATION:

Use string or cord to help make comparisons. For example, measure Mom's height with one piece of string and the child's with another; then lay the strings side by side on the floor to compare. Is Mom just a little bit taller or twice the child's height?

AN ADVANCED VARIATION:

If the learner appears ready for more advanced comparisons she might estimate and measure the perimeter or circumference of a variety of things. For example, is her head circumference greater or smaller than that of a selected adult? Is the perimeter of a tabletop more or less than that of a desktop or a bed mattress? Keep a record and compare these measurements. (*Note:* These measurements might be made with lengths of string or, for learners who are capable, with a measuring tape.)

Hand Guess

■ WHY DO IT?

To practice estimation and measurement with nonstandard units

To clarify measurement vocabulary (such as shorter and longer)

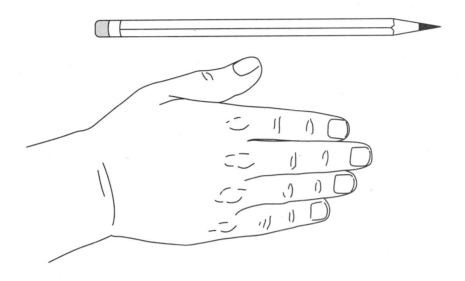

■ HERE'S HOW!

1. Make a record sheet like the one shown.
2. Have the learner estimate (guess) whether an object (perhaps a pencil) is shorter than, about the same length as, or longer than his or her hand.
3. Place the pencil beside the learner's hand and measure and compare. Discuss what he found out and then help him to record his answer on the record sheet.
4. Follow the same procedure with several items, such as a book, a can of vegetables, or a spoon.

SHORTER THAN	ABOUT THE SAME AS	LONGER THAN

ANOTHER VARIATION:

1. Have the learner use string to measure parts of her own body.
2. See if she can find another part of her body that measures about the same as the length of her foot, the circumference of her head, or the distance from fingertip to fingertip when her arms are stretched wide.
3. Help the learner to use words like shorter and longer as she makes comparisons; her findings might also be recorded in a chart such as the one shown.

ADVANCED VARIATIONS:

1. Have the learners try to find objects that are two of their hand lengths long, three hand lengths, four, and so forth.
2. Find the length of a room in the learners feet (toe to heel). Have an adult measure in the same way. Talk about why it takes more of their feet than the adult's feet to measure the same distance.
3. Help the learners keep a written record (perhaps as a picture and number journal) of their findings.

Footsteps for Fun

▪ WHY DO IT?

To practice estimation and measuring with nonstandard units

▪ HERE'S HOW!

1. Ask a learner to estimate how many of his feet are needed to measure a particular distance in a room. For example, at home he might determine how many feet it is from the television to the far wall. If done at school, he might estimate how many feet from the teacher's desk to his seat. Record the estimation.
2. Have the learner then measure off the distance by placing his left heel against the starting point, then placing his right heel to the toe of his left foot, and so forth. (*Note:* This requires physical balance, which some young children may have difficulty with.) Record the result.
3. Continue by having other learners estimate how many of their feet are needed to cover the same distance. Have them also record their findings after they have measured by walking heel to toe.
4. Have an adult measure the distance in the same manner.
5. Ask the learners about the differences in the number of feet measured. Talk about the reason for this.

▪ AN EASIER VARIATION:

1. Have the learner stand on cardboard or heavy paper and trace around his feet. Cut them out to make "footprints."
2. Let the learner measure several distances (such as the length of a table, the width of a room, the height of a chair) by placing his footprints heel to toe.
3. Have the learner tell you what he found out.

■ AN ADVANCED VARIATION:

1. Have several learners measure the distance between two points using their feet as the measuring devices. Record the results.
2. Measure the same distance using a standard 12 inch ruler. (*Note:* An interesting experience can be provided by having the learners wear size large men's thongs, which measure 12 inches long, as they pace off distances in heel-to-toe fashion.) Record the result.
3. Compare and discuss the differences.

Leaf Relief

WHY DO IT?

To practice measurement with nonstandard units
To make leaf art relief prints

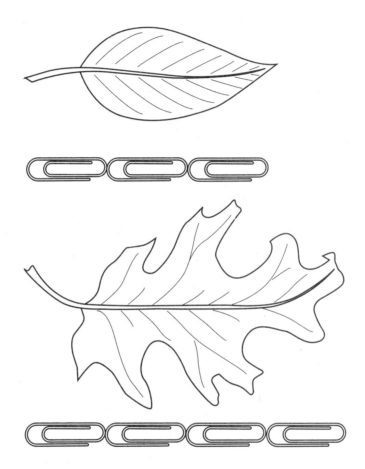

HERE'S HOW!

1. Have the learners collect a variety of leaves and make several leaf relief prints. To create a leaf relief print, place a leaf on a flat surface and under a sheet of paper; then rub the side of a crayon over the top.
2. Measure the length of each leaf relief print with paper clips placed end to end. Help the learner to write the length (in paper clips) below each print. Discuss which is the shortest; the longest. Put the leaf relief prints in order from shortest to longest.
3. If the learners remain interested, repeat the process using another unit of measurement such as pennies. Predict how many pennies it would take to measure each leaf. Then measure the leaves by placing several pennies in a row on top of each print. Discuss and record the findings.

■ AN EASIER VARIATION:

1. Collect a variety of leaves.
2. Compare the leaves by holding them next to each other. Talk about which is shorter, longer, and so forth.
3. Order the leaves from longest to shortest and glue them on a piece of paper in that order.

■ AN ADVANCED VARIATION:

1. Collect a variety of leaves.
2. Help the learner to measure the leaves to the nearest inch by laying them directly on a ruler (see Appendix A).
3. The learner should then keep a record of the measurements by gluing or making leaf relief prints of all the **1** inch leaves on one piece of paper, all the **2** inch leaves on another paper, and all the **3** inch leaves on a third paper.

Fill the Pan

WHY DO IT?

To develop volume relationship understanding

To practice counting in applied situations

HERE'S HOW!

1. Use a drinking glass and a pan.
2. Have the learner find out how many filled drinking glasses of water it takes to fill the pan.
3. Find a different size drinking glass and have the learner estimate (guess) whether it will take more or fewer glasses of the *new* size to fill the same pan. Then have the learner do it to find out.
4. Repeat the activity with larger or smaller drinking glasses.

AN ALTERNATE VARIATION:

1. Have the learners look at pots and pans of various sizes and shapes and predict which will hold the most water, the least water.
2. Help the learners fill the pans with water and pour from one to another as a check on relative capacities.

3. Have the learners put the pans in order from the one holding the least water to the one holding the most water. Also label them as number 1 for the pan holding the least, number 2 for the pan next in line, and so forth.

4. The learners might also practice using related math vocabulary words such as most, least, more, or less as they make clarifying statements. They might state, for example, "Pan 2 holds more than Pan 1" or "Pan 1 has less water than Pan 2."

■ AN EASIER VARIATION:

1. Provide three glasses or cups that are exactly the same size and shape. (*Note:* It will be easier to do this activity if you can see through the glasses.)
2. Have the learner fill each glass with a different amount of juice.
3. The learner should then compare how much juice is in each glass and put the glasses in order from least to greatest volume.
4. Have the learner explain why he placed the glasses in a particular order.
5. Finally, allow the learner to drink the juice in the cup of his choice.

■ AN ADVANCED VARIATION:

1. Obtain a standard tablespoon, a standard 8 ounce cup, a pint container, and a quart container.
2. Find out how many tablespoons there are in 1 cup by filling up the tablespoon repeatedly with water and pouring it into the cup. (*Note:* Make sure the learner knows that the water should be as level as possible in the tablespoon before pouring it into the cup.)
3. Continue by finding out how many cups are in a pint container; how many cups are in a quart container?
4. Can the learner find out how many pints are in a quart container?
5. As a further *challenge,* some learners might be able to determine the number of tablespoons in a quart.

Spoonful of Sugar

■ WHY DO IT?

To provide volume comparison experiences
To practice estimating volumes

Two, three, four...

■ HERE'S HOW!

1. Provide a teaspoon, a tablespoon, and a small cup (about one-half cup size).
2. Ask the learners to estimate (guess) how many level teaspoonfuls of sugar (or other dry ingredient) will fill the cup.
3. Count the number of level teaspoonfuls needed to fill the cup.
4. Ask the learners to find the numbers of teaspoons in a tablespoon and then ask them to estimate how many tablespoons will fill a cup.
5. Count the number of level tablespoons needed to fill a cup. Were the estimates close? Ask the learner to explain how he decided on the estimated number.

■ AN EASIER VARIATION:

1. Provide a variety of empty plastic containers and a small scoop. Ask the learner to fill each to the top with sand (or another dry ingredient such as cornmeal, rice, or beans). Count each scoop as it is poured. Talk about how many scoops each container will hold.

2. Have the learner make comparisons by pouring contents from one container to another. Discuss whether a container will hold the same amount, more, or less. Which container will hold the most, the least?

AN ADVANCED VARIATION:

1. Provide several containers that vary in shape but that have the same volume (hold the same amount).
2. Have the learners estimate the number of scoops of sugar each will hold and then experiment to find out. A tall slender coffee cup and a short fat one might both hold 8 scoops of sugar.
3. To verify the volumes of the containers, have the learners recount the number of scoops required and/or fill one and pour the sugar directly into the other.

ANOTHER ADVANCED VARIATION:

A further *challenge* might be to ask the learners to measure the number of tablespoons in a one-fourth cup measure. Then ask them to figure out how many tablespoons would be in a cup, in two cups, and so forth.

Mouth Full

■ WHY DO IT?

To have fun comparing mouthful capacities
To be exposed to "formal" volume measurement

■ HERE'S HOW!

1. Provide each learner with a large glass of punch and a straw.
2. Have each learner, in turn, use his or her straw to suck in a mouthful of punch.
3. When the learner's mouth is full, have her spit the punch into a see-through measuring cup or a graduated beaker.
4. Mark the level of punch on the measuring device with a small piece of tape containing the learner's name. Also record the volume (as 1/4 cup or 20 ml) on a piece of paper. Then empty the measuring device.
5. Use the same measuring device and repeat the activity for each learner. (*Note:* Limit groups to four learners so that the measuring device does not get too crowded with tape.)
6. When finished talk about whose mouthful was *biggest* and how we know.

■ AN EASIER VARIATION:

1. Provide each learner with a container of punch, a straw, and a see-through glass with his name on it.

2. Have each learner, in turn, use a straw to fill his mouth with punch.
3. When the learner's mouth is full, he should spit out the punch into his juice glass.
4. Line up the glasses on a table and compare the height of the punch in each glass.
5. Which glass has the most punch? The least? Whose mouthful was *biggest?*

AN ADVANCED VARIATION:

1. Give each learner a glass of punch and a straw.
2. Take turns having each learner use the straw to fill his or her mouth with punch.
3. When the learner's mouth is full, have him or her spit out the punch into a beaker that is graduated with milliliters.
4. Help the learner to read the scale on the graduated cylinder. He should also write down the amount of milliliters that his mouth holds.
5. Compare volumes to find out who has the biggest mouthful.
6. As an extension, ask the learners to find out how many of their mouthfuls it would take to fill a measuring cup (or another measuring device).

Up and Down Weights

◼ WHY DO IT?

To compare *heavier* and *lighter* weights

◼ HERE'S HOW!

1. Obtain or make a teeter-totter capable of holding children. (*Note:* You might balance a long board on a firewood log fulcrum or on several small boards nailed together.)
2. Make sure the teeter-totter balances with nothing on it.
3. Ask one learner to be the *standard* weight and sit on one end of the teeter-totter. (*Note:* Other objects, such as a large brick or a box full of sand, might also serve as the *standard* weight.)
4. Ask other learners to volunteer to be compared to the standard weight.
5. Help the learners to understand that people (or objects) lighter than the standard weight will go up on the teeter-totter, and that objects heavier than the standard weight will go down.
6. Help the learners record findings on a chart like the one shown:

LIGHTER things go up	Things ABOUT THE SAME balance	HEAVIER things go down

■ AN EASIER VARIATION:

1. Provide a variety of very heavy and very light objects for a learner to lift.
2. Have the learner pick up the objects one by one.
3. Discuss whether the object is heavy or light and how the learner's hand can easily go up while holding a light thing and how it wants to go down if holding a heavy object.
4. Place the objects in two categories: heavy and light.
5. Have the learner place the objects in order from heaviest to lightest.

■ AN ADVANCED VARIATION:

1. Make or obtain a pan balance. To make a pan balance, tape small containers, such as cupcake papers, to each end of a ruler and balance the ruler at its midpoint on a pencil.
2. Provide small objects for the learners to weigh and a standard weight object such as a washer or paperclip.
3. Let the learners discover which objects are lighter or heavier than the standard weight. Record the answers on a chart.
4. As an extension, have the learners find out how many standard weight objects it takes to equal heavier objects. Also record these outcomes in chart form and discuss the findings.

Lightweight/Heavyweight

■ WHY DO IT?

To begin comparing the weights of common objects by using nonstandard measurement units

■ HERE'S HOW!

1. Construct a milk carton scale (see illustration). Cut the bottom 1½ inches from a half gallon milk carton. Punch holes in all four sides and thread string through them. Attach the strings together at the top and loop or tie a large rubber band to the strings. Hang the milk carton scale from a ruler that is taped firmly to a bookshelf or countertop.

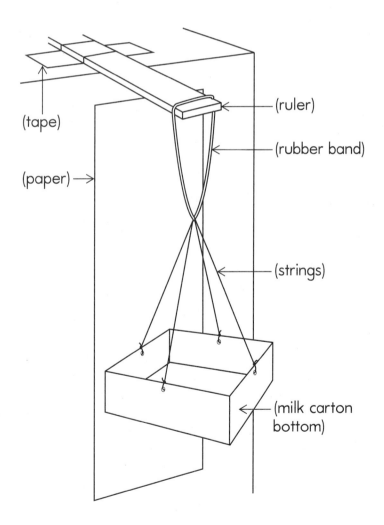

(tape)

(paper) →

(ruler)

(rubber band)

(strings)

(milk carton bottom)

2. Tape a piece of paper behind the scale and provide a variety of common objects (an apple, a glue bottle, a large crayon, soap) to weigh.
3. Have the learner hold the objects, compare them, and try to place them in order from lightest to heaviest.
4. She should place each item, in turn, on the milk carton scale.
5. Gently push the scale against the paper behind it and draw a line directly under the scale. Write the object's name or draw a picture of it on the line.
6. Repeat for all the common objects and talk about whether the original comparisons where correct.

AN EASIER VARIATION:

1. Make a milk carton scale using the directions and place a piece of paper behind it.
2. Provide a variety of two object sets that normally go together (such as a sock and a shoe, or a small mixing bowl and a large spoon, or a carrot and a celery stick). Also, provide sticky note cards (Post-it® Notes) with pictures of the objects already drawn on them.
3. Have the learner compare the related objects and predict which object is lighter, heavier, or if they weigh about the same?
4. He should then weigh one object at a time on the scale and place the matching sticky note on the paper directly under the bottom of the scale.
5. After each set of two related items has been weighed, talk about which is lightest or heaviest.
6. Repeat for each set of related objects.
7. As an extension, the learner might predict and find out if one item was a *lot heavier* or just a *little heavier*.

AN ADVANCED VARIATION:

1. Make a milk carton scale using the directions in Here's How above and place a piece of paper behind it.
2. Provide a set of nonstandard measuring units (such as metal washers, small tiles, or Unifix® cubes).
3. Place the washers or other objects in the scale until it lowers to the line of one of the common objects such as the apples.
4. Record the number of washers or other objects it took for the scale to reach the "apple" line on the recording paper. The student should keep a pictorial record (such as drawing 6 washers opposite the "apple").

What's Heavier?

■ WHY DO IT?

To relate the weight of objects to changes in shape

To compare items with the same volumes but different weights

To compare items with discrepant volumes and weights

■ HERE'S HOW!

1. Construct a milk carton scale (see illustration). Cut the bottom 1½ inches from a half gallon milk carton. Punch holes in all four sides and thread string through them. Attach the strings together at the top and loop or tie a large rubber band to the strings. Hang the milk carton scale from a ruler that is taped firmly to a bookshelf or countertop.

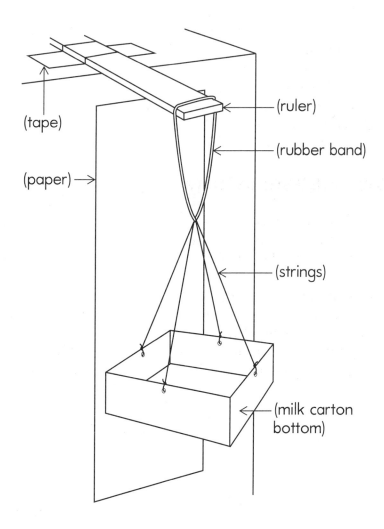

(tape)

(paper) →

(ruler)

(rubber band)

(strings)

(milk carton bottom)

2. Provide a container, such as a small cup, that will fit into the scale and tape a piece of paper behind the scale.

3. Provide different materials (such as rice, beans, water, sand, or seeds) that will be used to fill the cup.

4. Have the learner fill the cup with one material (such as the beans).

5. Place the cup on the scale and have the learner gently push the scale against the paper and draw a line directly under the scale on the paper. Label the material being weighed on that line.

6. Have the learner dump out the first material and put another material in the cup. He might predict whether the new material will be heavier or lighter than the first. Then have him measure the new item.

7. Repeat for all the provided materials. Then talk about the learner's predictions. Which materials were the heaviest? The lightest?

█ AN EASIER VARIATION:

1. Provide a milk carton scale and place a piece of paper behind it.

2. Also provide a ball of clay or Play Dough (see Appendix A for a recipe).

3. Have the learner place the clay ball on the scale, gently push the scale against the paper, and draw a line directly under the scale to show the weight.

4. Have the learner remove the clay ball, flatten it into a pancake shape, and place it back on the scale. (*Note:* The milk carton scale will extend to the same level.)

5. Have the learner remove the clay again and, this time, form it into a snake shape. Will the weight still be the same? Try it.

6. She should finally reform the clay into a ball and weigh it one more time. What happens now? Is the weight still the same? Talk about what she found out.

█ AN ADVANCED VARIATION:

1. Construct a milk carton scale and place a piece of paper behind it.

2. Also provide materials that vary widely in weight and volume (such as clay, Styrofoam®, a stapler, an empty cardboard box, a full Pepsi® can, an empty Pepsi can).

3. Hold up the Pepsi cans for the learners to see, but don't let them know one is empty. Ask which will weigh more, or will they be the same.

4. Use a milk carton scale to compare the Pepsi can weights. When the learners find out one was empty and object, ask whether everything that appears heavy or light actually is.

5. Continue by having the learners predict, weigh, record, compare, and talk about a wide variety of objects that might not weigh what is expected.

Time Stunts

◼ WHY DO IT?

To increase awareness of time intervals

◼ HERE'S HOW!

1. Talk with the learners about activities that take a relatively short amount of time to complete such as saying the ABCs, writing numbers to 10, jumping up and down 15 times, or singing "Twinkle, Twinkle, Little Star." Then select several activities to do.
2. Write each of the selected activities on a separate piece of paper and place it in a container.
3. Two players (or teams) each pick one activity from the container. The players then predict which of the two activities will take a shorter amount of time to complete. (*Note:* It is okay for both players to select the same activity.)
4. Each player (or team) then does his or her activity (the one drawn from the container) simultaneously to find out which activity actually takes less time to complete.

◼ AN EASIER VARIATION:

1. Provide a clock or watch with a second hand.
2. Select and try some of the following stunts for **1** minute each.
   Stand on one foot.
   Walk as far as you can.
   Count how many times you can bounce a ball.
   Count how many times you can jump rope.
   Count how many times you can touch your toes and then stand up.
   Count how many times you can snap your finger.
   Count how many times you can blink your eyes.

◼ AN ADVANCED VARIATION:

1. Provide a timer and, with the learners, select a period of time (such as 10 minutes, an hour) to be experienced.
2. Set the timer for the selected time period (perhaps 30 minutes). Have the learners predict how many 30 minute intervals will pass before a given event such as lunch, recess, or a favorite television show happens.
3. Keep track of how many times the timer goes off by making tally marks and then resetting the timer.
4. When the selected event happens, count the tally marks and have the learners talk about how close their estimate was.
5. Repeat the activity until the learners becomes quite accurate at predicting a reasonable number of time intervals.

Collecting Clocks

■ WHY DO IT?

To become more aware of time

To compare and contrast how clocks indicate time

■ HERE'S HOW!

1. Have the learners find and cut out pictures of clocks and watches from magazines and newspapers.
2. Focus initially on *hours only*. Help the learners identify the hour hand (or the hour portion of a digital readout). Help them to find several clock pictures that show the same hour.
3. Glue pictures of different clocks that show the same time on pieces of paper. That is, place all clocks showing 1:00 on one piece of paper, those showing 2:00 on another, and so forth.

■ AN EASIER VARIATION:

1. Cut out or draw pictures of things that happen in the daytime and in the nighttime.
2. Mix the pictures up and have the learners sort the pictures into daytime pictures and nighttime pictures.

■ AN ADVANCED VARIATION:

1. Provide both an easily read standard clock and a digital clock.
2. Set one of the clocks at an on-the-hour" time (perhaps 2 o'clock) and show the learner how to set the other clock to the same time. Repeat this activity for other hour times.
3. Trade clocks and repeat direction number 2.
4. If the learners appear ready for a further *challenge,* try having them work with half hours, or even with one minute intervals such as 3:10 or 4:27.

It's Time

■ WHY DO IT?

To relate time of day to clock time

To begin learning to read and write clock times

■ HERE'S HOW!

1. Show and talk about the different types of clocks and watches (include clocks with hands and those with digital readouts). Point out the 12 numbers on a standard clock face and note that each refers to an hour.
2. Discuss the fact that there is an 8:00 in the morning and also an 8:00 in the evening. (*Note:* Wait until later to introduce A.M. and P.M. concepts.)
3. Have the learner draw a picture of something he does at a specific time of the day. When the picture is finished, assist him in drawing a picture of a small clock in the corner that shows the hour this activity is done; also write the same time in digital format. The learner might, for example, draw a picture of eating breakfast; if this happens at 8 A.M. then both a clock face showing 8 o'clock and a digital readout of 8:00 should be added.

■ AN ALTERNATE VARIATION:

1. Help the learners to understand that the different types of clocks (digital readouts and standard clock faces) serve the same purpose but show times in a different manner.
2. Provide clock puzzle cards (shown below) with which they can practice matching times.

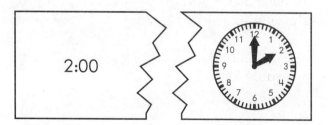 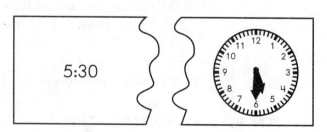

ANOTHER ALTERNATE VARIATION:

1. Use a paper clock (see clock pattern) to show the learners how the short hand indicates the hours. (*Note:* At first just the hour hand might be used. Later include the longer minute hand.)

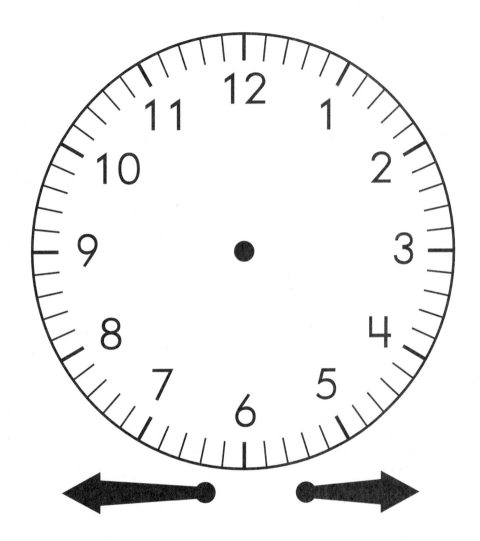

2. Give the learner a paper clock and have her match a whole hour time that you are showing on another clock. Be sure she notes the position of the hour and minute hands.
3. If the learner appears ready, state a whole hour time and have her show it on her paper clock. Later follow the same procedure for half hours.

AN EASIER VARIATION:

1. Read the book, *It's About Time Jesse Bear and Other Rhymes.*[1]
2. Talk about different activities done during the day and typical times for each activity such as eating lunch at 12:00 noon.

3. Personalize the activity by talking about the time a child typically gets up, goes to school, takes a nap, or goes to bed.

■ AN ADVANCED VARIATION:

1. Have the learners count the "minute spaces" around the clock face and note that there are 60 minutes in an hour.
2. Help the learners recognize and state time to the minute. As such, 3:10 might be stated as either "ten minutes after three" or as "three ten," and 8:45 should be either "forty-five minutes after eight" or "eight forty-five." (*Note:* It is suggested that the "quarter hour" and the "minutes until" designations be delayed until the learner is quite adept at telling time.)

■ ANOTHER ADVANCED VARIATION:

1. The learners should also compare standard clock face times with the same read-outs on digital timepieces.
2. They should then learn to write time in digital form (such as 3:00, 8:15, 10:42).

Time It and Graph It

■ WHY DO IT?

To gain an understanding of how long tasks take

To develop a conceptual understanding of minutes and seconds

■ HERE'S HOW!

1. Provide a stopwatch or a watch that displays minutes and seconds, graph paper (see Appendix A), crayons, and pencils.
2. Select a destination that each learner will take turns walking to and back (such as the length of a playground, or to the end of a block).
3. Have the learners take turns walking and timing how many minutes it takes each one to get to the designated site and return. (*Note:* Help the learners to *round* times of 30 seconds or more to the next minute.)
4. Show the learners how each block on the graph means 1 minute and how each learner's time is to be displayed in a single column. Then have each learner use an individual color to show his or her time on the graph (see example) and talk about the results.

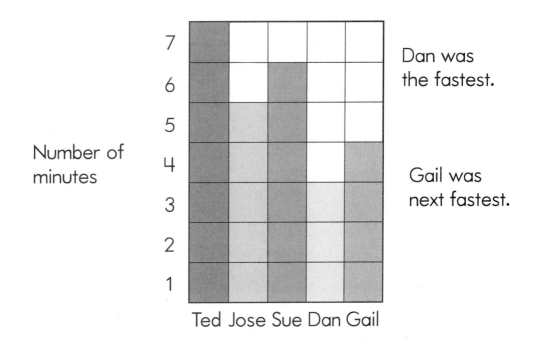

Number of minutes

Ted Jose Sue Dan Gail

Dan was the fastest.

Gail was next fastest.

■ AN EASIER VARIATION:

1. Provide a stopwatch or a watch that displays seconds, graph paper (see Appendix A), crayons, and pencils.
2. Select two places in a room that each learner will walk between.
3. Let each learner walk from point to point and time how many seconds it takes. (*Note:* An adult or older student may have to help read the watch.)
4. Help each learner to color in his or her time on the graph and talk about the results. Have the learners note why some people covered the distance more quickly than others. Does it have anything to do with how many steps the person takes, how long his or her legs are, and so forth?

■ AN ADVANCED VARIATION:

1. Provide a stopwatch or a watch that displays minutes and seconds, graph paper (see Appendix A), crayons, and pencils.
2. Select a safe destination (such as the length of a playground or to the end of a block) that each player will take turns walking to at regular speed, walking to as fast as possible, running to, and riding a bicycle to.
3. Time each player to the minute and second and have him or her plot the times for each event on a large graph.
4. Discuss the results. How much difference in time was there between walking at *regular* speed and walking as fast as possible? What was the difference in time when walking as compared with riding a bicycle?

Dressed for the Weather

■ WHY DO IT?

To understand relationships between temperatures and the appropriate clothing for various weather conditions

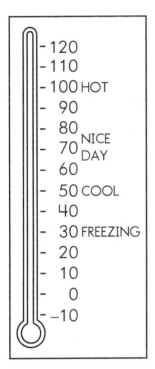 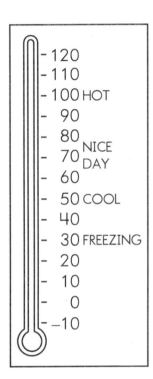 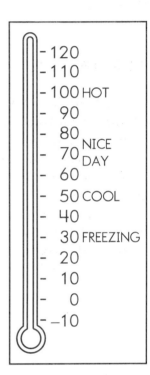 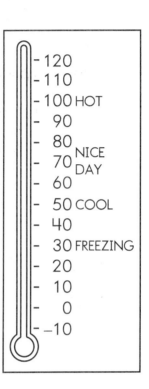

■ HERE'S HOW!

1. Provide a real thermometer (or photocopy the demonstration thermometers shown or see Appendix A for directions to make a ribbon thermometer) and discuss how the mercury goes up and down depending on the temperature. (*Note:* If using a real thermometer have the learner put his or her hand on the bulb to raise the temperature reading and put the thermometer in cool water to lower it.)
2. Have the learner imagine that he is at the beach on a hot day and talk about what he would likely be wearing.
3. Have the learner fold a piece of paper in half. On one half he should draw a picture of what he would be wearing for a day at the beach. On the other half draw a thermometer or glue on a thermometer copy from above and show that day's temperature by coloring in the mercury strip.

4. Choose three or four more weather conditions, such as days when it is raining, snowing, partly cloudy, or sunny. Talk about likely temperatures on such days and have the learner complete clothing and thermometer pictures for each.

5. As an extension, cut and separate the thermometers from the clothing pictures. Mix them up and have the learners rematch them.

■ AN EASIER VARIATION:

1. Find pictures of people in different climates (from magazines, newspapers, the Internet) and provide a ribbon thermometer (see Appendix A for directions) or use a demonstration thermometer.

2. Select one of the pictures and have the learners move the temperature strip on the ribbon thermometer (or color in the mercury strip on a thermometer copy) to show what the approximate temperature would be where the person is. Ask them to explain their reasoning.

■ AN ADVANCED VARIATION:

1. Tell the learners to imagine that they are going to take an imaginary vacation. Tell them what the weather and temperature is like at each of their destinations (*Note:* If able, have the learners research their own vacation destinations to find out about the weather there.)

2. Have the learners then list or draw pictures of what they would pack in suitcases for their trip.

3. As an extension, the learners might be asked to use a Celsius thermometer scale (or consider both Fahrenheit and Celsius temperatures) when dealing with such tasks.

Hot and Cold

▨ WHY DO IT?

To better understand the measurement of daily temperatures

To practice recording and comparing temperature measurements

▨ HERE'S HOW!

1. Have the learners observe an outdoor thermometer. Help them read and record the temperature each day at approximately the same time. (*Note:* A good place to keep this record is on the calendar.)
2. At the end of each week, discuss which day was the hottest and which was the coolest.
3. Keep a record for an entire month. Discuss what the temperatures were like on days that were sunny, cloudy, windy, and so forth. Mark the hottest and coldest days. Was there a large difference in temperature or were the days similar?

▨ AN EASIER VARIATION:

1. Discuss the concept of hot and cold temperatures. Introduce the thermometer as a device used to measure temperature by reading the story *Is It Cold Enough for a Sweater?* by Sydney Dickson.
2. Help the learners to make paper thermometers (see Appendix A for directions) and ask them to move the red mercury line to indicate colder and warmer temperatures.
3. Have the learners observe temperature differences by placing thermometers in different areas of a room. For example, the temperature on a sunny window sill will likely be different than that in a closet, the area near the ceiling will likely be warmer than that at floor level, and so forth. Talk about why there are such differences.
4. Use the paper thermometer to *show* the temperatures from each area. Talk about where the warmer (or colder) temperatures were found, and so forth.

▨ AN ADVANCED VARIATION:

1. Keep a record of the temperatures at your location for a week or longer.
2. Read and/or listen to the weather reports provided in the daily newspaper and on radio and television.
3. Talk about why the *official* temperature might differ from the temperature at your location. What other weather differences might there be?
4. Help the learner find out how many degrees difference there was each day between the *official* temperature and the temperature at your location.

Is It Cold Enough for a Sweater?

Sydney S. Dickson

Jerry and Jan were ready to leave the house to catch the school bus when they heard mother say, "You better take a sweater with you, its rather cold outside."

"But the sun is shining," called Jerry, "that means it's warm."

"Not all the time," said mother, "take a look at the thermometer and see what the temperature is."

Jerry looked at the thing mother called a thermometer that was hanging outside the kitchen door. He shrugged and said, "I'm looking at it, but I don't know what it means."

"I'll be right there," said mother. "I'll try to explain it to you. Come with me, Jan, you might be interested in this too."

Mother showed the children the numbers and the red line on the thermometer. She explained that the red line goes up and down when the temperature changes. Even though she didn't know the scientific reasons, she knew that warm temperatures warmed the liquid in the thermometer and made it expand or get bigger. This squeezed the liquid upward. When the temperature outside cooled, the liquid dropped down. "The red line in this thermometer is probably colored alcohol," she said, "but others have mercury inside that is a silver gray color."

Mother explained that during the winter when the weather is cold, the thermometer's red line is short and stays near the bottom where the numbers are low. As the weather begins to get warmer, the red line grows longer and longer until sometimes it reaches numbers that are at the top of the thermometer and may be as high as 100 or more. The days are very hot when it is 100 degrees.

Jan thought for a minute then said, "Grandpa has a thing on his house that he looks at to tell how hot it is, but it is round and has an arrow thing on it. Is that a thermometer too?"

Mother smiled and said, "That is a good question, Jan. You're correct; Grandpa's thermometer is different from ours but it still tells the temperature. I wish I could explain the mechanical differences to you. Maybe we can go to the library and look up a book that will explain it to all of us. For now, lets see if you can read the temperature on our thermometer."

Jerry and Jan looked closely at the numbers. They saw large numbers that ended in zero and five and there were little lines between them. Mother said to count the lines and when they did, they decided there were four lines between the 50 and the 55. Jerry looked at the thermometer, "I think the red line is up to 53 this morning," he said.

"You are absolutely right," said mother. "We say, the temperature is 53 degrees. I think that is chilly enough for you to wear a sweater. You may not need to wear it when you come home from school, because temperatures often go up in the afternoon." Jerry and Jan got their sweaters from the closet and told mother they would look at the thermometer when they came home from school to see if it changed.

That afternoon when they arrived home, the children checked the thermometer and the red line was definitely higher. In fact, it was up to 71 degrees. Jan said, "You were right mother. We don't need our sweaters now."

Mother asked if anyone wanted a freshly baked oatmeal cookie. "Yes!" the children said together and raced for the kitchen. While they ate a cookie, Jan told mother how she shared the thermometer story with her class at school. Her teacher talked more about thermometers and temperature during math and they learned about some different places where thermometers are used. Her teacher explained they are in refrigerators and freezers to make sure they are cold enough and also in an oven to make sure it is hot enough to cook things like cookies. Jerry said his class also talked about thermometers, and he learned that a special type is used to take people's temperatures to see how sick they are.

Later that evening, when dad heard Jerry and Jan's story about thermometers, he suggested they watch the news and weather on television and look at the weather information in the newspaper. It was interesting to see how temperatures are different in towns only a few miles away. Jerry and Jan decided to keep a record of the temperature at their house. They planned to look at the thermometer in the morning before they went to school and again when they came home in the afternoon, and write the temperature on the calendar. Then they would look in the newspaper and find the temperature in the town where their grandpa lives. Dad suggested they keep track of how much hotter or colder it was in their town than where grandpa lives.

That night before they went to bed, Jerry and Jan checked the thermometer again. The red line was going down. It was getting cooler than it had been in the afternoon. They agreed it had been an interesting day. Maybe tomorrow they would check the school library to see if they could find a book that explained more about how thermometers work.

Measure Me

◼ WHY DO IT?

To practice measurement using whole inch and centimeter rulers

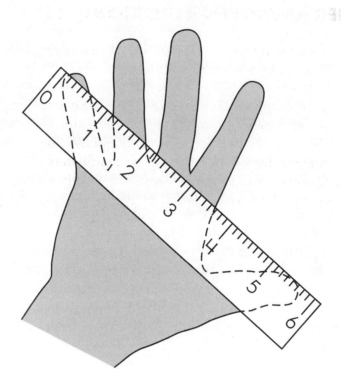

◼ HERE'S HOW!

1. Have the learners trace their hands on a piece of paper.
2. Using an inch or centimeter ruler (see Appendix A), help them measure their hands. Measure the length from the base of the palm to the tip of the middle finger and the span from the end of the thumb to the end of the little finger.
3. Record each measurement.
4. The learners might also wish to measure other body parts (feet, toes, nose).

◼ AN EASIER VARIATION:

1. Have the learners compare hand sizes by measuring against each other's hands. Are all hands the same size?
2. Trace the learners' hands on a piece of paper. Using the inch ruler, help them measure their hand lengths and spans and record the findings. (*Note:* This information might be kept in order to show growth between the beginning and end of a year.)

■ AN ADVANCED VARIATION:

1. Help the learner use the centimeter ruler (see Appendix A) to measure the length and span of his hand.
2. Make the same measurements with an inch ruler.
3. Compare the results and talk about the differences.

■ ANOTHER ADVANCED VARIATION:

1. As a *challenge,* the learners might be asked if they are "square"; not in everyday terms, but mathematically square?
2. Then work together to measure each learner's height and width. To determine width each learner needs to stand with arms extended at shoulder height while a partner uses a piece of string to measure from the tip of one middle finger across the chest to the end of the other middle finger.
3. Record the results in inches or centimeters.
4. Compare each person's height and width measurements. Are they the same or very nearly so?

Works Cited

1. Nancy Carlstrom, *It's About Time Jesse Bear and Other Rhymes* (New York: Macmillan, 1990).

CHAPTER 4

Geometry

We experience geometry in many areas of our daily lives; sometimes in realms we never think of as geometry. We use it in construction, sewing, art, product packaging, mapmaking, and reading. The ideas of symmetry are found in architecture, sports, and clothing design as well as throughout nature. We use spatial thinking when giving, receiving, and following directions and while using charts and diagrams to assemble toys or furniture.

Young learners come to school with some beginning geometric or spatial notions. In order to further such understandings, these young learners need many additional opportunities to see and manipulate two- and three-dimensional shapes and to talk about their properties. As such, they will begin to make comparisons and understand relationships. In time, they will also learn the shape names and identify their uses in man-made settings and in nature.

A variety of geometry activities are provided in this chapter. They range from informal/intuitive experiences, to understanding the characteristics of shapes found in everyday life, to discerning the interrelationships both within and among figures, to utilizing geometry in creative ways. These activities will serve as a basis for spatial thinking and for discussions between children and parents and children and teachers.

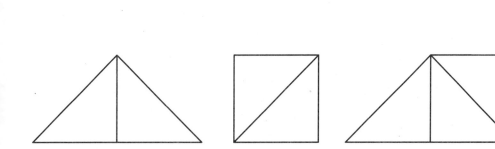 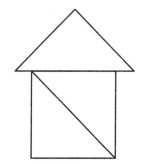

Food Patterns

■ WHY DO IT?

To become more aware of naturally occurring patterns

To expose learners to naturally occurring fractions

■ HERE'S HOW!

1. Provide an orange, a lemon, and a grapefruit.
2. Cut the fruits into halves (midway between top and bottom).
3. Have the learners compare the segments of the different fruits. Are the patterns similar? Which has more segments? Are all the segments about the same size?
4. Cut two of the same type of fruit (such as two oranges) and compare their patterns.

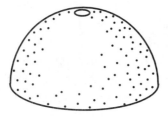 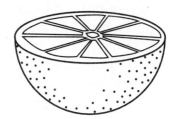

■ AN EASIER VARIATION:

1. Collect different fruits and vegetables such as apples, oranges, cabbage, onions, and eggplant.
2. Cut the fruits and vegetables into halves (midway between top and bottom).
3. Have the learners look at the patterns in each and draw a picture of the patterns or designs they see.

■ AN ADVANCED VARIATION:

1. Provide an orange, a lemon, and a grapefruit.
2. Cut the fruits in half (midway between top and bottom).
3. Talk about fractions with the learners by looking at how many sections it takes to make a whole orange, a lemon, a grapefruit. If an orange has ten sections then 10 out of 10 or 10/10 would be a whole orange. If you were to eat 1 section, that would be 1/10 of that orange. If you were to eat 3 sections, what fraction of the orange would that be?

Search for a Shape

WHY DO IT?

To recognize basic geometric shapes in familiar surroundings

To increase awareness of such concepts as straight and curved lines, corners, sides, edges, and so forth

HERE'S HOW!

1. Have the learners search for and find items that are shaped as squares, rectangles, triangles, and circles.
2. The learners should record on a chart the items found as shown. They might do so by drawing simple pictures of the items and/or an older student or an adult might help write the words for the items.

SQUARES	RECTANGLES	CIRCLES	TRIANGLES
(floor tile)	(my bed)	(soda can)	(pie server)

■ AN EASIER VARIATION:

1. Provide the learners with a cut out shape such as a circle.
2. Search for items in school or at home that have a circle shape. Compare the items found with the cut out shape.
3. Have the learners record their answers by drawing *simple* pictures of the items found.

■ AN ADVANCED VARIATION:

1. Have the learner locate shapes made of straight lines and others that have curved lines. Talk about the number of sides, the number of corners, and the names for a variety of shapes. (*Note:* It is okay to use alternate terms such as "side," "edge" and "border," or "corner," "vertex," and so forth, but, for the most part, keep it simple for young learners.)
2. Make a chart like the one shown.
3. Pick an item in the room such as a couch and determine which categories the item belongs in. Does it have any straight lines? Curved lines? Corners? Write the word "couch" or draw a picture of the couch under each heading where it belongs.

STRAIGHT LINES	CURVED LINES	CORNERS
(back of couch)	(arm of couch)	(arm meets the back)

Shape Draw

■ WHY DO IT?

To show and identify different geometric shapes

To recognize and copy patterns

■ HERE'S HOW!

1. Have the learners make and color pictures with at least three circles, three squares, three rectangles, and three triangles in each.
2. Then trade pictures, find the different shapes, and talk about them.

■ AN EASIER VARIATION:

1. Cut several circles and squares from colored paper. Design a simple pattern and have the learners continue it.
2. Add a third shape such as a triangle and design a more complicated pattern for the learners to duplicate.
3. When the learners understand the concept of patterns, ask them to design a pattern for you or a friend to copy.

■ ANOTHER EASIER VARIATION:

1. Photocopy the shapes shown and have the learners color and cut them out, making sure that at least two of each shape are of the same color. For example, the smallest and middle-sized squares might be colored red, while the largest square is colored blue.
2. Ask the learners to pick up one shape and then find another shape that is similar to the one just picked.
3. Repeat the process until all the shapes have been worked with.
4. Finally, have the learners find cutouts that are the same shape and color.

■ AN ADVANCED VARIATION:

1. Make two squares, two circles, two triangles, and two rectangles from poster board or cardboard.
2. Place the shapes in a bag.
3. Have the learner feel in the bag without looking and hold onto a shape.
4. The learner must feel, tell what the shape is like (such as it has 2 long straight sides and 2 short straight sides), and name the shape without looking.
5. She then pulls the shape from the bag and everyone checks and talks about the attributes of that shape.
6. The shape is then returned to the bag for the next learner's turn.
7. As a challenge, ask the learner to feel in the bag and find two shapes that are the same. Then ask her to show and identify the shapes and tell why they match.

Traffic Sign Shapes

■ WHY DO IT?

To recognize different shapes used in our everyday world

To note how traffic signs promote safety

■ HERE'S HOW!

1. Have the learner inspect the traffic signs shown below.
2. Identify which signs are circles, squares, rectangles, and triangles. Also talk about what each sign is telling us.
3. While riding in the car or on the bus, have the learner look for the different traffic signs. Ask the learner to tell about the shape of each sign and what it means.

■ AN EASIER VARIATION:

1. Photocopy the traffic signs shown here and assist the learner as he cuts them out.
2. Discuss the sign shapes and meanings with the learner.
3. Ask the learner to group the signs that are circles, squares, triangles, and rectangles. (*Note:* Young learners may need help with triangles and rectangles that are not identical because they will likely look different to them. When this happens, point out the attributes of each shape. For example, all triangles have three sides.)
4. Encourage learners to look for traffic signs when they are in the car or on the bus and point them out.

■ AN ADVANCED VARIATION:

1. Have the learners identify the traffic signs shown.
2. What are some other traffic signs that are not shown here? Are any of them a different shape? (One commonly seen sign that has eight sides is the STOP sign.)
3. When riding in the car, have the learners identify and keep a record of the different traffic signs they see. They should make a tally mark each time one is seen and, at the end of the trip, total the marks for each sign. Which sign was seen most often?

Shape Picture

WHY DO IT?

To become familiar with the names of basic shapes

To increase spatial awareness

HERE'S HOW!

1. Photocopy the shapes shown and help the learners cut them out.
2. Ask the learners to identify each shape, show where on the butterfly it belongs, and then glue it onto a separate paper to make their own butterflies.
3. To extend the activity, have the learners identify and cut out more shapes and create a picture or design of their own with them.

AN EASIER VARIATION:

1. Photocopy the shapes and help the learners cut them out.
2. Have the learners talk about, match, and glue the shapes directly onto the picture of the butterfly.

AN ADVANCED VARIATION:

1. Provide real life examples (photographs or pictures cut from magazines) of objects in our world that are made with basic geometric shapes. As examples, microwave ovens, doors, and chalk boards are often rectangles; dinner plates, clocks, and globes may be circular; floor tiles and some cake pans are square; pie servers and construction braces are frequently triangles.
2. Have the learners look at the pictures and point out the different shapes they see. Also take a walk and see if they can point out more examples.

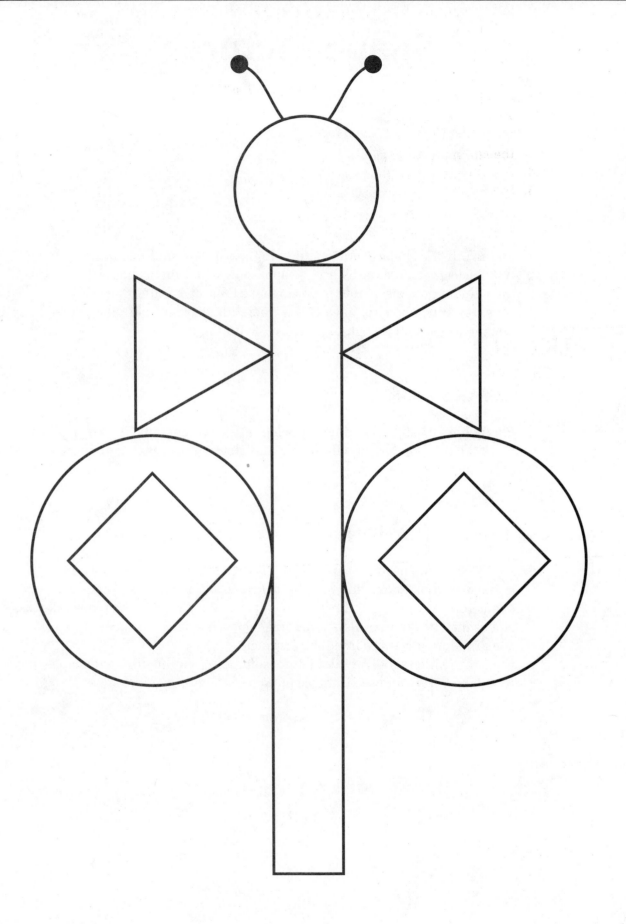

Is It Symmetrical?

■ WHY DO IT?

To increase understanding of symmetry (having a mirror image)

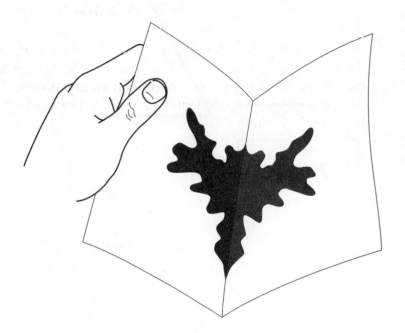

■ HERE'S HOW!

1. Ask the learner to fold a sheet of paper in half.
2. Instruct the learner to open the fold and put a small blob of paint on one side of the paper.
3. Have the learner refold the paper and rub the top gently with his hand.
4. The learner should then reopen the paper and tell what he sees. Are the images on the left and the right sides of the paper the same? Are they symmetrical? (*Note:* Young children may need help with the terms "left" and "right," and especially with "symmetry" or "symmetrical." Do expose them to such words/concepts, as they are often intrigued, but don't expect mastery.)

■ AN EASIER VARIATION:

1. Find simple pictures such as a face or a vase of flowers or anything that is symmetrical in design.
2. Cut the picture so that each half is symmetrical and have the learner put the two pieces together.

3. Have the learner place half of the picture against a mirror and look at the mirror image. Does the image in the mirror look like the cut out half picture? Allow the learner to experiment with several different images.

■ AN ADVANCED VARIATION:

1. Take a walk around the house or school and look for objects that are symmetrical. Examples might include lamps, a television set, or chairs. Ask where the objects would have to be cut in order for the halves to be symmetrical (the lines of symmetry).
2. Make a list of at least ten items that could be cut to create symmetrical halves.
3. As an extension, ask the learners to find items that are not symmetrical? These are called "asymmetrical." An example of an asymmetrical item is a coffeepot. Make a list of several asymmetrical items you find and describe or draw a picture of how they are different.

Alphabet Symmetry

WHY DO IT?

To help understand geometric symmetry (mirror images)

HERE'S HOW!

1. Pick a capital letter from the alphabet, such as an *A*.
2. Draw a line down the middle of the letter; then examine the halves to see if they match.
3. Try the same procedure with several other capital letters. Keep a record of those that are symmetrical.
4. You may want to let the learners use a mirror (place it standing up on the middle line) to check their answers. Letters that are symmetrical will project a mirror image even though half of the letter is blocked from view.

AN EASIER VARIATION:

1. Make paper cutouts of several capital letters, fold each letter down the center, and draw a line on the crease.
2. Give an unfolded letter to each learner. Have the learner guess whether each side of the letter would match exactly if it was again folded on the line.

3. Have the learner check by refolding that letter on the center line and physically seeing whether it is symmetrical or not.
4. Repeat the process with several other letters.

AN ADVANCED VARIATION:

1. Help the learner discover which letters are symmetrical when the center lines are drawn horizontally and when the center lines are drawn vertically.
2. Make paper cutouts for all of the symmetrical capital letters and cut them in half.
3. Give the learner one half of a letter at a time. She should then try to determine which letter it will be when matched with its identical half.
4. Have the learner find the matching letter piece, place the halves together, and check to see if she *guessed* correctly.

Pattern Production

■ WHY DO IT?

To provide spatial sense experiences

To develop spatial/positional vocabulary (above, to the right of, and so forth)

To practice following and giving positional directions

To identify and extend geometric patterns

■ HERE'S HOW!

1. Color and cut out pattern pieces such as yellow triangles, blue squares, red ovals, green rectangles, and orange circles.
2. Divide the pieces equally between two players.
3. Put a divider, such as a large book, file folder, or box, between the players so they cannot see each other's pieces.
4. Player #1 makes a *hidden* design with all or some of the pieces. (Keep the designs simple at first.)
5. Player #1 then helps Player #2 attempt to build an identical design. He does so by stating the appropriate color and shape names together with position words such as "right," "left," "next to," "above," "below," and so forth.
6. After Player #2 has listened and built what she thinks to be an identical design, the divider is removed and the designs are compared.
7. An extension, to be used when the players become better at describing and following directions, is to *drop* the color descriptions and use only the shape names.

■ AN EASIER VARIATION:

1. Review the names and attributes of some basic geometric shapes such as circles, triangles, and squares.
2. Cut out five or more of each shape from paper (use only one color to begin with).
3. Produce a simple repeated pattern (begin with just two shapes such as □□○-□□○-□□○). Then have the learner copy the pattern by placing the same shapes directly above (or even right on top of) the provided pattern.
4. Next, ask the learner to extend the pattern several times (for example □□○-□□○-□□○-□□○-□□○-□□○).
5. After successfully copying and extending several two- and three-shape patterns, ask the learner to design a new pattern, explain it, and then extend it several times.
6. If a further *challenge* is desired, take turns designing and solving increasingly more complex patterns.

PATTERN PRODUCTION PIECES

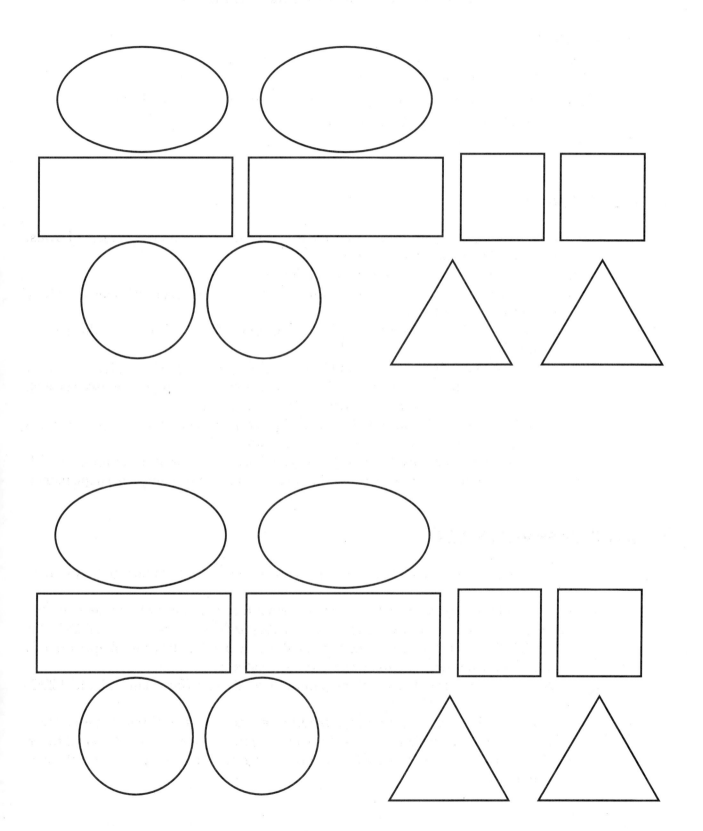

■ AN ADVANCED VARIATION:

1. Using the shapes below as patterns, cut out several sets of the five or more geometric shapes (such as circles, squares, rectangles, triangles, ovals, and so forth) from several colors of paper.
2. Have two players take turns as they work together. To begin, Player #1 should design a pattern for Player #2 to view.
3. Player #2 must then determine if the design is really a repeated pattern. If so, she needs to reproduce and continue it for two complete repeats.
4. After reproducing the pattern with paper pieces, Player #2 should record the pattern by using crayons or colored pencils to draw it on paper.

Shape Design

■ WHY DO IT?

To gain experience with spatial relationships

To have fun designing and solving puzzles

■ HERE'S HOW!

1. Photocopy the square and have the learner cut it into five individual pieces as marked.
2. He should then use all five pieces to cover the arrow.

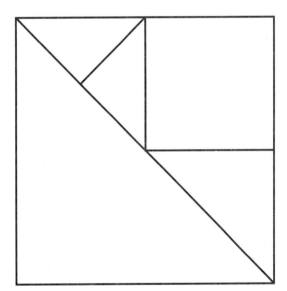

SHAPE DESIGN ARROW

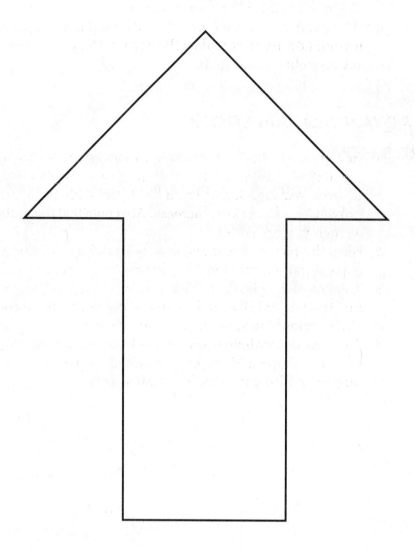

■ AN ALTERNATE VARIATION:

1. Have the learners use all five pieces to make their own shape designs and trace the outlines carefully.
2. Have the learners exchange this new design outline with a friend and have the friend try to fit all five pieces into the new shape design.
3. Make several more design outlines and try to solve them.

■ AN EASIER VARIATION:

1. Before cutting the square into five pieces, photocopy or trace an identical figure on another sheet of paper.

2. Then carefully cut the square into five individual pieces as marked.
3. Have the learner match the pattern by putting the cut pieces on top of the same shape in the traced or copied square.
4. As a *challenge,* put the pattern out of sight, mix up the five pieces, and have the learner now try to complete the square. (*Note:* If the learner has difficulty, she can ask for help.)

AN ADVANCED VARIATION:

1. Have two or more players each take an 8½ × 11 sheet of paper and divide it into segments by using a ruler and drawing a variety of straight line shapes such as squares, rectangles, and triangles. (Start with 10 to 15 shapes and expand to approximately 25 as skills increase. Also note that the individual pieces must be large enough to work with.)
2. Have the players use crayons or felt markers to color a design on one side of the paper and then cut along the drawn lines to create the pieces.
3. Then have the players exchange pieces, use another sheet of paper as a base to define the original size, and try to put the puzzle back together again.
4. Use envelopes to store the individual shape puzzles when not in use.
5. As a further *challenge,* the pieces from one puzzle might be arranged into an interesting shape and traced around. Then ask another player to try to solve the puzzle by filling it in with the cut shapes.

Using Right Triangles

■ WHY DO IT?

To manipulate and identify geometric shapes

To locate triangles in everyday settings

To create new shapes from triangles

■ HERE'S HOW!

1. Photocopy and cut out the four triangles below.
2. Have the learner arrange the triangles to make a square, a triangle, and a rectangle.
3. Have the learner cut out more triangles. How many does it take to make a bigger square, triangle, or rectangle?

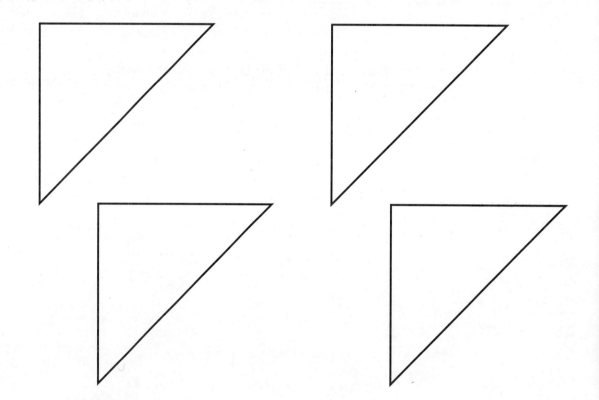

■ AN EASIER VARIATION:

1. Have the learners compare different types of triangles (any three-sided figure). How are they alike? How are they different?
2. Have the learners find triangle shapes in the room.

■ AN ADVANCED VARIATION:

1. Have the learner keep a record of what she was able to create with two triangles, 3 triangles, and so forth. She should do so by tracing the figures she created. (*Note:* Provide help as needed with holding the figures in place as they are traced.) The learner may be able to find more than one outcome for each situation as shown.

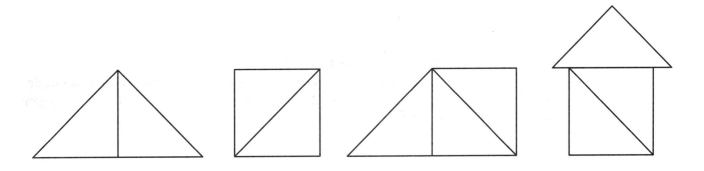

2. Have advanced learners use the chart shown to keep an organized record of findings.

CAN YOU DO IT?

Can you make a: When using:	triangle?	square?	rectangle?	another shape? (draw it)
1 triangle				
2 triangles				
3 triangles				
4 triangles				
5 triangles				
6 triangles				
7 triangles				
8 triangles				
9 triangles				
__ triangles				

Which Way Is "Right"?

◼ WHY DO IT?

To develop spatial awareness skills

To practice giving and receiving directions when using words such as "left," "right," "in front," "behind," "over," "under," "on top," and so forth.

◼ HERE'S HOW!

1. Provide the learner with two different colored blocks such as blue and red.
2. Direct the learner to place the blue block on the right side of the red block.
3. Then ask, which block is on the right side? The left side?
4. Repeat the activity by placing the blocks in varied positions and using words such as "behind," "in front," "under," and "on top" to specify locations.

◼ AN EASIER VARIATION:

1. Trace the learner's left hand on a piece of paper and label it "left." Tape that sign to the left side of a table.
2. Trace the learner's right hand on a piece of paper and label it "right." Tape that sign to the right side of the same table.
3. Then, using the direction words "left" and "right," ask the learner to place objects on the table. He might, for example, place a book on the right side of the table or put a glass on the left side of the table.

◼ AN ADVANCED VARIATION:

1. Provide the learner and a partner with a barrier such as a large book and objects of the same size, shape, and color, such as blocks.
2. Have Player #1 place three blocks on the table touching each other, but behind the barrier so that the other player cannot see them. The blocks may be stacked or placed side by side or behind each other or in any combination.
3. Player #1 must then give directions (using the words "left," "right," "under," "on top," and so forth) to Player #2 so that she can build a structure that is exactly like that of Player #1.

◼ ANOTHER ADVANCED VARIATION:

Play "Simon Says" using right and left parts of the body such as "Wave your right hand." You may even want to get complicated by saying things like "Touch your right elbow to your left knee."

All Around Walk

■ WHY DO IT?

To practice using the directions left, right, forward, and backward

To increase spatial concept understandings

■ HERE'S HOW!

1. Provide an *All Around Walk game board,* markers for each player (such as a bean, a button, a nut or a bolt) and a paper clip spinner (see directions in Appendix A).
2. Place the markers for all the players on the "Start Here" center square of the game board and have everyone sit on the same side.
3. Each player takes turns spinning the spinner and moving his or her marker one space in the direction the spinner shows.
4. The first player to move her or his marker off the board wins.

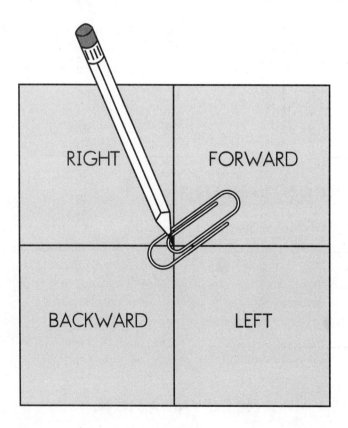

MAKE A SPINNER: Lay a paper clip so that one end overlaps the center point of the chart above. Put a pencil point through the loop end of the paper clip and hold it on the center of the chart. Use your other hand to spin the paper clip.

ALL AROUND WALK GAME BOARD

			START HERE			

◼ AN EASIER VARIATION:

1. Use chalk to draw a large 7×7 square grid (big enough for people to stand in the squares) or use masking tape to mark off such an area on a tile floor.
2. Label the sides of the area with the words "left," "right," "forward," and "backward."
3. Have the players act as their own markers by standing in the center square of the area and facing in the same direction to begin (so that the words "left" and "right" on the board will be correct).
4. Each player then takes turns spinning the spinner and physically moving one space in the direction the spinner shows.
5. The first player to step off the board wins.

◼ AN ADVANCED VARIATION:

1. Use an 11×11 grid (or larger) and two spinners—one to designate direction and another to tell whether to move 1, 2 or 3 spaces. Also provide markers for each player.
2. Each player then takes a turn spinning the spinners and moves his or her marker 1, 2, or 3 spaces in the direction indicated.
3. The first player off the board wins.
4. As a greater *challenge,* map-type directions (such as North, East, West and South; perhaps even Northwest, Southeast, and so forth) might be used. As such a player might be directed to move 2 spaces North or 1 space Southwest, and so forth.

Hide and Seek

■ WHY DO IT?

To increase spatial awareness

To practice following and giving positional directions

To develop spatial/positional vocabulary (left, right, near, far, beside, and so forth)

■ HERE'S HOW!

1. Player #1 hides an object, that is about 4 to 6 inches tall, in the room or outside while Player #2 covers his eyes.
2. Player #1 then gives directions to aid in finding the object such as "straight ahead" or "go left" or "make a square turn to the right." Player #2 must then do exactly what the first player has directed as he seeks the object.
3. Once the object has been found, have the players change roles so they both experience following and giving directions.

■ AN EASIER VARIATION:

1. Provide a small object and a box that is large enough for the object to fit into.
2. Have an adult place the object in various locations in relation to the box, such as in the box, behind the box, to the right of the box, and so forth.
3. Ask the learner to tell you where the object is in relation to the box.
4. When the learner feels confident, ask her to identify a location in relation to the box and place the object there. This demonstrates understanding of position words.

■ AN ADVANCED VARIATION:

1. Provide Post-its® or index cards of three different colors (such as white, blue, and yellow). Write large size numbers 0–9 on the white cards, alphabet letters on the blue cards and post them at two foot intervals along two perpendicular walls (begin with the cards for letter A and number 0 in the corner). Then write sequential clues on the yellow cards and post them in their proper coordinate positions. (*Note:* It saves some confusion if the clue cards are labeled Clue 1, Clue 2, and so forth.)
2. Place the first clue card at position (A,0) and have it read something like, "You are at position (A,0) and this is Clue Card 1. You will find Clue Card 2 at position (D,5). See if you can find it and the other clue cards that follow. Good Luck!"
3. The players must try to find, in order, all of the clues. (*Note:* If desirable, a small prize might be provided for successful completion.)

3-D Shape Search

■ WHY DO IT?

To become aware of everyday three-dimensional shapes
To identify and give clues about three-dimensional shapes

■ HERE'S HOW!

1. Show the learners a cube, a cone, a cylinder, and a sphere (ball). Talk about the special characteristics of each of these 3-dimensional (3-D) shapes (such as that the faces of a cube are all flat and square).
2. Then go on a *3-D Shape Search* walk. Walk around the neighborhood or go to a grocery store and identify 3-D shapes.
3. Talk about the kinds of shapes located, where they were found, and record at least one of each shape (by listing or drawing a rough picture of each item).
4. The learners might also be asked which 3-D shapes were man-made? Nature-made?

■ AN EASIER VARIATION:

1. Let the learners hold and talk about several 3-D shapes and then put them into a box.
2. Have each learner reach into the box without looking, feel one of the objects, and tell about it.
3. The learner should then take the object out, hold it up, tell about the characteristics, and name it. (*Note:* Provide help, if needed, in naming the object and/or in clarifying the characteristics.)
4. Replace the object and have the learner take another turn.

■ AN ADVANCED VARIATION:

1. Go on a 3-D Shape Search walk.
2. Take turns playing *I Spy*. Give clues that refer to 3-D shapes that were discussed earlier. The student might say, for example, "I spy a very tall cylinder. It is brown and sticks into the ground. The cylinder is solid and holds up wires. What is it?"

2-D, 3-D

■ WHY DO IT?

To become aware of similarities and differences in geometric shapes

To note how two-dimensional shapes serve as the faces of many three-dimensional objects

To learn the names of two- and three-dimensional shapes

■ HERE'S HOW!

1. Collect a set of two-dimensional (2-D) geometric shapes and their matching three-dimensional (3-D) counterparts. For example, the counterparts for a circle might be either a sphere (ball) or a cylinder (can) and those for a square might be a cube (box).
2. Discuss the names of both the 2-D and 3-D objects with the learner; also look for items in the environment that are similar.
3. Place the 3-D objects in a box or bag so the learner cannot see them.
4. Then have the learner reach into the box without looking, feel the object, tell what 2-D shapes the faces feel like, and name the matching 3-D shape. (*Note:* If this proves to be too difficult, place the 2-D shapes on a table and ask the student to point to the shape that matches the 3-D shape she is feeling in the bag.)
5. As an extension, provide the learner with several 3-D objects and have her trace around the faces. (*Note:* Use a pencil to trace the faces of small objects on paper and chalk to trace large images on a sidewalk.) Then ask the child to identify the matching traced 2-D shape outline.

■ AN EASIER VARIATION:

1. Select a variety of objects such as jar lids, washers, keys, coins, puzzle pieces, and so forth.
2. Help the learners to make an outline drawing of each by tracing around the items on a piece of paper or poster board.
3. Place the objects in a box or bag and shake to mix them up.
4. Then ask the learners to match the items with the proper outlines and to place them on top of their line drawings as a check.
5. As a *challenge,* the learners might be asked to work with objects that have similar but just slightly different shapes.

■ AN ADVANCED VARIATION:

1. Collect a variety of 3-D items such as cans, boxes, foods, vases, and so forth.
2. Arrange the objects as a still life art group.
3. Then have the learners use colored pencils, crayons, or markers, to draw a picture of this still life.
4. When finished, have the learners compare the actual 3-D grouping with their own 2-D drawings. How are they similar? What differences can be noted?

Building Frameworks

■ WHY DO IT?

To gain experience with spatial relationships

To design and build geometric frameworks

To logically analyze everyday geometric structures

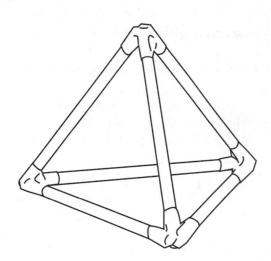
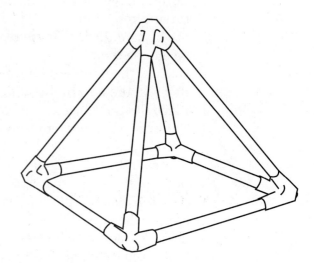

■ HERE'S HOW!

1. Provide newspapers, plastic straws (3 inches or longer), and tape.
2. Have the learners construct 10 or more long slender cylinders by taping a straw to the corner of each newspaper sheet (see illustration), rolling it tightly, and taping the resulting paper cylinder in two or three places. Also fold over and tape each end for added strength.
3. Have the learners first construct two-dimensional frameworks by taping the cylinders together at their ends. They might make triangles, squares, or pentagons. As they do so, ask how many sides or edges each has and what each is named?
4. Next, have the learners construct three-dimensional frameworks that are *large* and *neat*. To do so they must tape the cylinders together at their ends in order to form frames for triangular-based pyramids, square-based pyramids, and so forth (see examples).
5. If a cube is attempted, the learners will likely have difficulty. They will discover the need to reinforce the cube with several triangles in order to achieve stability.

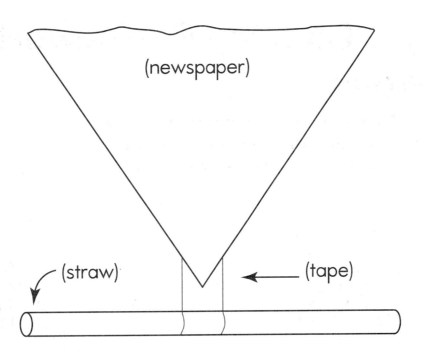

AN EASIER VARIATION:

1. Provide newspapers, plastic straws (3 inches or longer), and tape.
2. Help the learners construct several cylinders by taping a straw to the corner of each newspaper sheet (see illustration), rolling it tightly, and taping the resulting paper cylinder in two or three places. Also fold over and tape at each end for added strength.
3. Help the learners construct two-dimensional frameworks such as triangles, squares, and pentagons by taping the paper cylinders together at their ends. Talk about the number of sides each has and tell what each is named?
4. If the learners appear ready, help them to construct a three-dimensional framework such as a triangular-based pyramid. Young children especially enjoy such *large* and *neat* structures.

AN ADVANCED VARIATION:

1. Have the learners begin by building a basic three-dimensional framework, such as a tetrahedron (triangular-based pyramid). To do so, follow the initial instructions as noted earlier.
2. Then extend their experiences and understanding by also having them construct and analyze more complex frameworks such as those for an octahedron, or a do-decahedron, or perhaps even an icosahedron. (*Note:* Since the learners likely will not know of these figures, they may need help in doing some research about them.)

3. Finally, ask the learners to classify information about these more complex frame-works in a chart such as the one shown.

	FACE TYPE	NUMBER OF FACES	NUMBER OF EDGES	NUMBER OF VERTICES
Tetrahedron	triangle	4	6	4
Hexahedron	square	6		
Octahedron		8		
Dodecahedron		12		
Icosahedron		20		

CHAPTER 5

Problem Solving and Reasoning

 problem-solving situation is one in which a person wants something and does not immediately know what to do to get it. As such, real-world situations and events that make sense to young learners are often the best starting points. When taking part in such investigations young learners should also be exposed to reasoning/logical thinking skills.

Careful reasoning or logical thinking may generally be thought of as a way to make good sense out of something, usually in an organized way. When dealing with investigations, learners might be helped to:

1. Identify exactly what the problem is.
2. Tell what information is already known.
3. Decide on a plan of attack.
4. Collect needed information.
5. Organize the information and look for patterns.
6. Talk about what has been found out so far and, if necessary, change the plan.
7. Persist; allow for more time and extended effort.
8. Produce a report or product that describes or explains the findings.

This chapter provides a variety of problem-solving and reasoning activities appropriate for young children. Included are investigations involving estimation, sorting, logic, patterns, sounds, and probability. Furthermore and finally, it is hoped that these activities will serve as a basis for important discussions between young learners and parents and between these learners and their teachers.

Toy Sort

■ **WHY DO IT?**

To develop logical thinking abilities

To sort items according to similarities, differences, and uses

■ **HERE'S HOW!**

1. Have the learners collect a number of toys.
2. They should then sort the toys and put them in different locations. For example, put all the stuffed animals on the bed, all sports equipment on a rug, all trucks on a shelf, all dolls on the chair, and so forth.
3. After talking about why they sorted the toys as they did, ask them to sort them in a different way. As such they might put the dolls and the stuffed animals with the trucks and explain that they sometimes get to ride in the trucks.

■ **AN EASIER VARIATION:**

1. Provide the learners with an assortment of small items.
2. Ask them to place the items in groups that are alike. (They might put buttons in one group, paper clips in another group, and coins in another group.)
3. Talk with the learners about why they placed the items in the way they did.

AN ADVANCED VARIATION:

1. Together with the learners look through magazines and cut out pictures of items that go together such as animals or food or modes of transportation.
2. Ask the learners to first classify the items into large groups such as foods or vehicles for transportation.
3. Then ask that the items be further classified. Foods might be sorted as vegetables, fruits, or meats. Transportation vehicles might be classified as those for travel on roads, in the air, or on water.
4. As a further *challenge,* the subgroups might even be classified further. The learners might consider, for example, vehicles that have two, three, four, or more wheels; or those, like automobiles, that are motorized, and those that are not, such as bicycles.

Follow the Leader

WHY DO IT?

To recognize, use, and analyze patterns

HERE'S HOW!

1. With the players facing each other or in a circle, start a hand pattern such as clap, clap, wave; clap, clap, wave, and so on.
2. The other players copy this pattern until the leader changes it.
3. Choose another leader and have him or her start a different pattern.

AN EASIER VARIATION:

1. With the players facing each other or in a circle, clap a pattern (such as three claps).
2. The next players must then copy the pattern (echo clapping).
3. If the players are capable, vary the clapping pattern by number of claps and rhythm (such as 1 slow, then 2 fast). Try several combinations as long as the players remain interested.
4. Determine whether each learner understands such patterns by having everyone take a turn as the leader.

AN ADVANCED VARIATION:

1. Have players take turns developing patterns that use a variety of body movements. A player might begin, for example, by clapping four times, stomping her foot twice, and turning around.
2. The other players must then repeat the pattern three times.
3. Encourage creativity as each player takes a turn at being leader. At his turn one leader might, for example, jump high, turn a complete circle, bow and sit down.

ANOTHER ADVANCED VARIATION:

1. Have an individual (or a small group) make up and perform a *round* of rhythm sounds that will grow into a rhythm orchestra.
2. After demonstrating the round of sounds several times, ask another person (or small group) to join in, at a designated point, and keep repeating the pattern.

3. Additional people (or small groups) might also be asked to join in as the *round* is continued.

4. Have the learners notice the differences in sound as each additional person or group is added.

5. Conclude by having the first individual or group stop and then each subgroup drop out in sequence when each has completed the pattern.

6. As groups drop out, again note the difference in sound.

7. As an extension, the learners might be helped to notice exact rhythm patterns, codify them, and talk about the related mathematical patterns. (As examples, a pattern like clap, clap, snap, snap could be coded as *A, A, B, B* and counted as 1, 2, 3, 4 and considered as 4 quarter notes; whereas another with movements as slow-step, slow-step, jump, jump, jump, jump might be coded as *A-A, A-A, B, B, B, B* and counted as 1–2, 3–4, 5, 6, 7, 8 and considered as 2 quarter notes followed by 4 eighth notes.)

Sound Patterns

WHY DO IT?

To recognize sound patterns

To actively reproduce sound patterns

To recognize, reproduce, and develop sound (and physical) patterns

HERE'S HOW!

1. Start a sound pattern by saying "Buzz, buzz, ding, buzz, buzz, ding, buzz, buzz, ding."
2. Have the learner keep the same sound pattern but change the sounds that are being used. The above sound pattern, for example, might be changed to "Shhh, shhh, pow, shhh, shhh, pow" or "Oink, oink, meow, oink, oink, meow."
3. Extend the experience by trying more difficult sound patterns.

AN EASIER VARIATION:

1. Begin with a simple two-sound pattern such as "Zing, dong, zing, dong."
2. Have the learners join in when they know the pattern.
3. Extend the sound pattern to one that has sounds repeated twice such as "Thud, thud, ping, ping, thud, thud, ping, ping" or to patterns that repeat as one sound, then two, such as "Baa, naa, naa, baa, naa, naa."
4. In each instance have the learners join in when they know the pattern.

AN ADVANCED VARIATION:

1. Use patterns with the learners that can have both sounds and physical actions associated with them.
2. Have the learners attempt a pattern such as clap, clap, step, step, clap, clap, step, step. As such they must say "clap, clap" and at the same time clap their hands twice, and then say "step, step" and simultaneously take two steps.

Pine Needlely Patterns

WHY DO IT?

To learn to recognize, repeat, and extend patterns

HERE'S HOW!

1. Gather pine needles (or use toothpicks, pens, or pencils).
2. Have Player #1 begin a pattern with the pine needles. Then Player #2 must try to continue that same pattern.
3. Allow each player to take a turn at beginning a pattern.
4. As an extension, ask the players to show what the pattern would look like if it were rotated 90 degrees, if it were placed upside down, and so forth.

AN EASIER VARIATION:

1. Gather a bunch of pine needles.
2. Set out a simple pattern with the needles, such as the one below.

3. Have the learner make an exact copy right below the original pattern.
4. Try several patterns and, if the learner appears ready, make them increasingly more complex.

■ AN ADVANCED VARIATION:

1. Have the learners try to complete number patterns such as the following:

    1, 2, 3, 1, 2, _____ , _____ , _____ , _____ ,

    2, 4, 6, 8, _____ , _____ , _____ , _____ ,

    1, 4, 7, 10, _____ , _____ ,

2. If the learners appear ready, they might make up a number pattern and have another person try to figure out what comes next.

Silverware Sort

■ WHY DO IT?

To develop the ability to see similarities and differences

To deal with everyday problem situations

■ HERE'S HOW!

1. Dump the silverware from its drawer or use plastic knives, spoons, and forks and have the learner sort the silverware by utensil type.
2. Have the learner count how many of each type of utensil there are and keep a record of that information (with numbers or tally marks).
3. Then ask questions such as:

   What do we have the most (or least) of?

   How many more spoons than forks do we have?

   Do we have enough silverware to have ten people over for dinner? Why or why not?

■ AN EASIER VARIATION:

1. Dump the silverware from its drawer or use plastic knives, spoons, and forks.
2. Have the learner sort the silverware, show that she has all of the same type of utensil together, and put the silverware back into the drawer.

■ AN ADVANCED VARIATION:

1. Do the original activity noted earlier. Then have the learner figure out how many more pieces of silverware would be needed in order for there to be the same number of each utensil.
2. After arriving at a solution in one way, ask that he also find another way to solve the problem. The learner might accomplish this by counting, or addition, or subtraction, or he might compare the utensils on a 1-to-1 basis by lining up all the forks in one row and then all the spoons in a row right under the forks and matching them.

Classifying Collections

■ WHY DO IT?

To develop logical thinking abilities

To classify items according to similarities and differences

To keep records with Venn diagrams

■ HERE'S HOW!

1. Provide a collection of buttons, pencils, bolts, or rocks for the learners to inspect.
2. Sort the collection according to a *secret* rule and have the learners try to guess the rule. (A simple rule might separate pencils that have erasers from those that do not.)
3. After solving for several rules, have the learners make up rules of their own and have other players try to guess the new rules.

■ AN EASIER VARIATION:

1. Provide a collection of items that are quite different from each other, such as buttons, pencils, feathers, bottle caps, and cotton balls, and have the learner divide them into related groups (classification).
2. The learner should then explain why she grouped them as she did. (She might have, for example, grouped the bottle caps, pencils, and buttons as "hard items" and classified the feather and cotton balls as "soft items.")
3. After finding and talking about one rule for grouping, ask the learners to find another way to group the same items.

■ AN ADVANCED VARIATION:

1. Have the learner pick 1 object, such as a large red button with 4 holes. Then place objects that differ from it in only one way in separate groups, and explain why this was done. The results might display a group that has large red buttons with 2 holes; another with buttons that have 4 holes and are large, but are not red; another that contains small red buttons with 4 holes; and so forth.

2. Have the learner use overlapping loops (Venn diagrams) to classify objects according to their attributes. The example shows how pencils might be classified. In this case, the pencils are sorted as to whether they are *yellow* and/or *long* and/or have an *eraser*. Notice that where 2 loops overlap the pencils must have 2 and only 2 similarities.

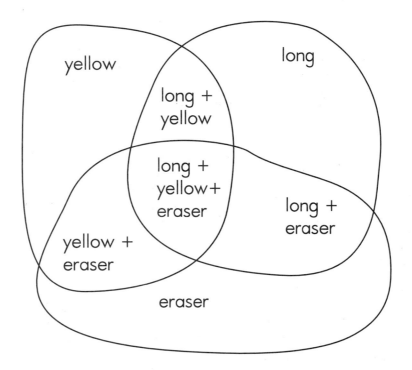

Attributes in Common

■ WHY DO IT?

To practice recognizing common (shared) attributes

■ HERE'S HOW!

1. Ask the learner to name something that is like a cat.
2. He should then tell what *it* is and why it is like a cat. If a rabbit was picked, for example, he might say they are alike because they both have fur.
3. Have the learner then think of other things that are like a cat in the same way (they have fur) and then things that are like a cat in a different way. He might note, for example, that an owl and a cat are alike because both have two eyes.
4. Have the learner also look for common attributes for other items (such as a car or a book or Cheerios® or a ladybug).

■ AN EASIER VARIATION:

1. Name three related things such as a car, a truck, and a bus.
2. Have the learner tell you what the three things have in common (such as you can ride in them or they all have wheels).
3. If the learner is successful, she might be asked about other *related* items such as an orange, a basketball, and a pearl, or a squirrel, a cat, and a mouse.

■ AN ADVANCED VARIATION:

1. Secretly choose an attribute (such as long sleeves) common to several learners in the group and pick one learner with that attribute to come to the front of the room.
2. Have the players guess who else might be able to join the first person. (*Note:* Only if a person selected has long sleeves will he or she be allowed to come up.)
3. After three or four learners are in the front of the room, allow the remaining players to take turns trying to guess what attribute they all have in common.
4. Select other attributes, such as blue eyes, tie shoes, has red on, short hair, and extend the activity. Also, allow the learners to select "secret" attributes and try them with each other.

Cupboard Rearrange

WHY DO IT?

To categorize items using different criteria

To develop spatial awareness skills

HERE'S HOW!

1. Help the learners take out all the items from a cupboard at home or at school.
2. Have them rearrange all the items (for a specific reason) and place them back in the cupboard. For example, put all the canned vegetables together, or arrange the items from smallest to largest, or put all items for lunch on a selected shelf.
3. Have the learners explain why they placed the items where they did.

AN EASIER VARIATION:

1. Have the learner practice matching. Begin with a collection containing several sets of identical items that are in mixed order. Have the learner locate and match the items by placing them side by side. For example, placed in pairs might be two cans of green beans and two boxes of Jello® brand strawberry gelatin dessert mix.
2. To make the task more complicated, add similar items such as a box of another brand or flavor of gelatin desert. Ask the learners to explain how the items are similar and how they differ. This will help them to begin noting when items are similar but *not* identical.

AN ADVANCED VARIATION:

1. Have a *rule* in mind and arrange items accordingly. For example, place the canned goods in a stack with those having the greatest diameters at the bottom, or arrange items in a sequence like boxed item, sacked item, canned item, boxed item, or arrange the items by weight. The learner must then guess and explain the rule.
2. On the learners' next visit to the grocery or hardware store have them notice the placement of items. Discuss how they are grouped. Are they in the *best* location or would another be better? Why?

What's Missing?

■ WHY DO IT?

To recognize mathematical patterns

To determine missing pattern elements

■ HERE'S HOW!

1. Ask the learners to listen carefully as you say a series of five numbers (such as 1, 2, 3, 4, 5).
2. Then repeat the number series, but leave one number out (1, 2, 3, 5).
3. Ask the learners to tell you which number was missed.
4. Repeat the activity with other number sequences.

■ AN EASIER VARIATION:

1. Draw a color pattern on a piece of paper, such as red dot, blue dot, red dot, blue dot, red dot, blue dot.
2. Then hide the dots with your hand and place a penny (or another small object) over one of the dots.
3. Ask the learner to tell which color dot is covered up by the penny.
4. Hide the dots with your hand again, move the penny to a new dot, and have the learner tell you which dot is now covered.
5. Extend the activity by drawing a slightly more difficult pattern such as red, red, blue, red, red, blue, and again ask the learner to try to identify the covered color.

■ AN ADVANCED VARIATION:

1. Photocopy the *Hundred Number Board*.
2. Have the learner color all the tens (10, 20, 30, and so forth) blue and then have him write the number sequence 10, 20, 30, and so forth on a different piece of paper.
3. Cover one of the numbers in the tens' sequence and have the learner tell you which number is covered. (He may try to guess with or without looking at the *Hundred Number Board*.) Cover a different number in the tens' sequence (or even several numbers at once) and try again.
4. Try the same activity with other number sequences (such as 2, 4, 6, 8, 10) making sure to always show the learner the pattern on the *Hundred Number Board* as he begins.

HUNDRED NUMBER BOARD

1	2	3	4	5	6	7	8	9	10
11	12	13	14	15	16	17	18	19	20
21	22	23	24	25	26	27	28	29	30
31	32	33	34	35	36	37	38	39	40
41	42	43	44	45	46	47	48	49	50
51	52	53	54	55	56	57	58	59	60
61	62	63	64	65	66	67	68	69	70
71	72	73	74	75	76	77	78	79	80
81	82	83	84	85	86	87	88	89	90
91	92	93	94	95	96	97	98	99	100

Scavenger Hunt

■ WHY DO IT?

To locate and classify everyday items according to similarities and differences

■ HERE'S HOW!

1. Prior to beginning the *Scavenger Hunt,* decide with the learners on attributes that will be used to limit their search. It might be decided, for example, that the search categories will be "brown" and "smaller than a television" and "both".
2. As the learners find matching items, they should list them (or draw a picture of each) in a chart such as the one shown.

BROWN	BOTH	SMALLER THAN A TV
	jewelry box	fork

3. When finished, have the learners talk about how the items are similar and/or different.

■ AN EASIER VARIATION:

1. Have the learner fold a piece of paper in half from top to bottom and label one side *red* and the other *not red*. Then have the learner make lists (or draw pictures) and talk about the *red* items and the *not red* items she was able to locate at home or in school.

2. As an extension, have the learner classify things in other ways. For example, she might find, list, picture, and talk about items that are *shorter, taller,* or the *same* height as she is.

■ AN ADVANCED VARIATION:

1. Have the learners use the information from the original Scavenger Hunt activity and create a Venn diagram with it (see below).

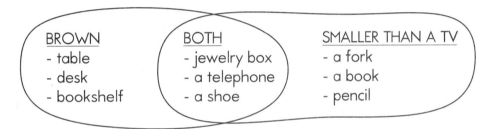

2. As a further challenge, ask the learners to create a Venn diagram for three or more attributes. In the example shown, the learners are looking for things that are smaller than a soccer ball and/or that can be talked to and/or that use numbers to make them work and/or that can be listened to and/or any combination of these.

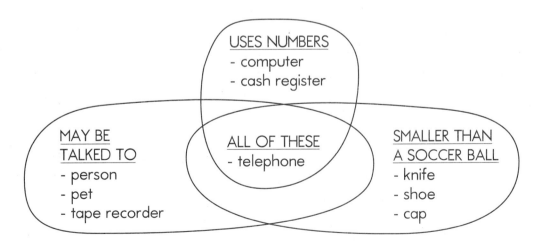

Across the Board

■ WHY DO IT?

To develop strategies and encourage logical thinking

To use language to describe logical strategies

■ HERE'S HOW!

1. *Across the Board* is a strategy game for two players.
2. Provide four markers for each player (one player might use four beans, another four green buttons, and so forth) and a game board.
3. To begin, each player must place his or her markers along an edge of the game board (one player to an edge).
4. In turn, each player must move one of his or her markers a single space forward, backward, left, or right, but not diagonally, into an open game board square. (*Note:* Two players may not occupy the same space.)
5. The winner is the first player to move all of his or her markers across and off the board. (*Note:* Talk about strategies that might lead to success.)

AN EASIER VARIATION:

1. *Get to the Win Box* is a game for two players.
2. Provide three or four markers (buttons or beans) and a strip of paper (adding machine tape works well) that has been divided and marked into 10 or more spaces. Also write the word "Win" in the far left-hand square (see below) of the game strip.
3. Player #1 begins by placing the markers anywhere along the strip with one marker in a space.
4. Player #2 may then, as spaces are available, move a marker one or two spaces, following these rules:
   - *No space may have more than one marker in it.*
   - *Markers may not be jumped over.*
   - *Markers must always be moved left toward the "Win" box.*
5. Players take turns attempting to move one marker at a time toward or into the "Win" box. If a player moves a marker into the "Win" box, he or she scores a point. (If the markers are eatable items, such as cereal, minimarshmallows, or peanuts, the players might be allowed to eat their winnings.)

AN ADVANCED VARIATION:

1. *Secret Code* is a game of logic for two. Success depends on problem solving by the player who is the **code breaker** and is based on feedback from the **code maker.**
2. Photocopy the game boards (as shown) and cut out small paper squares (each must fit on an individual game board grid space) of four different colors plus black. Decide how many games will be played before beginning.
3. The code maker decides on a pattern using any four colored squares and secretly puts it on his or her *Secret Code* game board (which the code breaker cannot see).
4. The code breaker then makes a first attempt at *breaking* the *Secret Code* by placing four colored paper squares on selected grid spaces of his or her game board.
5. The code maker then gives feedback by placing a black square above any column where the placement is correct. He must also verbally announce any other colored markers that are in correct columns, but in a wrong position. (*Note:* In the sample below, the code breaker has placed *red* in the proper row and in the proper space, as indicated by the black square placed above that column; *blue* is in the proper column, but in a wrong position; *pink* and *tan* are both in wrong columns and positions.)

6. The code breaker then uses the clues and tries again. Play continues until the code has been broken and is correctly reproduced.
7. When the *Secret Code* has been solved, the players should be encouraged to talk about strategies and then change roles and play again.

Code Breaker
(first try)

RED			
	BLUE		
		PINK	
			TAN

Code Maker

RED			
		TAN	
	BLUE		
			PINK

The Critter Crawl

WHY DO IT?

To develop logical reasoning skills and strategies while playing games on 2-dimensional boards

HERE'S HOW!

1. Photocopy the *Critter Crawl* board and provide a die or spinner with the numbers 1, 2, 3 and 1, 2, 3 on it (see Appendix A), and Critter markers (or photocopy and cut out those shown).
2. Each player (up to 4) places his or her critter marker on a different side of the board.
3. Player #1 rolls the die and states the number rolled. She then moves that many squares horizontally and/or vertically. (*Note:* A player rolling a 3 might move 2 spaces vertically and 1 horizontally.) Player #2 then takes a turn. (*Additional Notes:* Two critters may not occupy the same square and barriers may not be crossed.)
4. Play continues with the players taking turns around the board. The first critter to reach the opposite side wins.

AN EASIER VARIATION:

1. Provide a checker board, one critter marker for each player (up to four players), and a spinner or die with the numbers 1, 2, 3 and 1, 2, 3 on it (see Appendix A).
2. Also cut out six small paper barriers (each should be 2 or 3 spaces long). Fold them so that they will stand and have the players place them on the checker board (three horizontally and three vertically).
4. Then play the game as described above.

AN ADVANCED VARIATION:

1. Provide a die numbered 1 through 6 and four playing pieces such as 4 pennies, 4 buttons, or 4 paper clips for each player.

2. Play the game as first described above, except that players may land on a square that contains an opponents playing piece. If a player lands on an opponents piece, she gets a bonus turn.
3. The first player to get all of his or her pieces to the other side of the board wins.

CRITTER CRAWL BOARD AND PIECES

Penny Pickup

■ WHY DO IT?

To develop logical thinking skills
To look for winning patterns

■ HERE'S HOW!

1. Place ten pennies in a line.
2. Each player, at his or her turn, must remove either *one* or *two* pennies. (If, for example, Player #1 takes 2 pennies, eight are left. Player #2 then takes 1 penny and seven remain. Player #1 next takes 1 penny and six are left. Player #2 takes 2 pennies, leaving four. Player #1 again takes 2 pennies and leaves two. Player #2 takes the remaining 2 pennies and wins because he took the last two pennies.)
3. The player who picks up the last one or two pennies wins.
4. After two or three games talk about *winning* strategies. When just three pennies remain, who will win? When four pennies remain? How about five or six pennies?

■ AN EASIER VARIATION:

1. Place five pennies in a row.
2. At each turn a player may take only one penny.
3. The player to take the last penny wins.
4. Play several games, switching who takes the first penny. Does a certain player always win? Ask the players to explain why?

■ AN ADVANCED VARIATION:

1. Play the original activity with 10 or 15 or more pennies.
2. Instruct the players to take turns removing one, two, or three pennies.
3. Have the players talk about who will win and in which situations? Is there a pattern to "winning"?

Last Is Best

■ WHY DO IT?

To play games that encourage strategy development
To develop logical thinking and problem-solving skills

■ HERE'S HOW?

1. Photocopy the *Last Is Best Game Board* shown. Players are to take turns placing markers in either one or two triangles on the board. No one may skip a turn.
2. If a player, at his or her turn, chooses to place two markers, the areas in which they are placed must connect on a *full* edge (see examples).

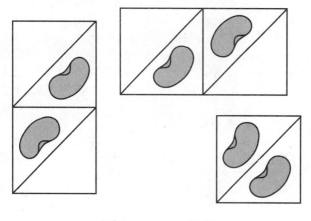

These are O.K.

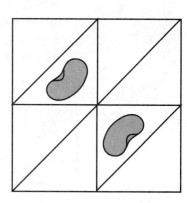

This is NOT allowed

3. The last person to fill in a triangular area wins! (*Note:* If desired, the *Last Is Best Game Board* might be expanded in size.)

THE LAST IS BEST GAME BOARD

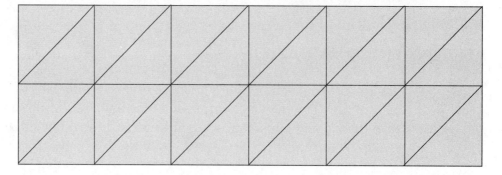

AN EASIER VARIATION:

1. Provide a game board (a 7 × 7 sample is shown) and different markers for each of two to four players.
2. Have them play *Three in a Row* (a Tic-Tac-Toe type game). To begin, each turn a player must place one of her or his markers on the game board. Then, as subsequent turns are taken, each player tries to get three markers in a row (horizontally, vertically, or diagonally).
3. The player to get three markers in a row the most times is the winner.
4. For players who appear ready, *challenge* them to reverse the object of the game. That is, as they play they need to avoid getting three markers in a row.

THREE IN A ROW GAME BOARD

AN ADVANCED VARIATION:

1. Play the *Mancala* version of the ancient game *Kalaha*. (*Note:* At first the game appears confusing, but one or two practice moves will help players become familiar with the rules and allow them to concentrate on strategies. The rules are simple but the tactics for winning take time to master.)
2. The game can be played with a lidless egg carton, two small containers (boxes or custard cups), and 36 small objects (beans, beads, popcorn kernels). Place the two small containers at the ends to serve as the players' scoring pods. The sections of the egg carton are playing pods, with each player having one side as his or her home territory.
3. Begin by placing three small objects such as beans in each of the twelve playing pod sections of the egg carton.

The initial game board for *Mancala* is illustrated here.

Player #2 (sits here)

(Scoring Pod for Player 2)	:·:	:·:	:·:	:·:	:·:	:·:	(Scoring Pod for Player 1)
	:·.	.·:	:·.	.·:	:·.	.·:	

Player #1 (sits here)

4. Player #1 chooses one of her pods and takes the three *seeds* to sow, one at a time, in successive pods moving around counterclockwise.
5. If the last seed in a play is placed in that player's own scoring pod, she gets another turn.
6. If the last seed is placed in an empty pod on her own side, she then captures the seeds in the opposite (the opponent's) pod.
7. All captured seeds, as well as the last seed played, are taken out of the playing pods and placed in the player's own scoring pod.
8. The game ends when all pods on one side of the egg carton are empty.
9. Each seed becomes a point. The player with seeds remaining puts them in his or her own scoring pod. The player with the most seeds is the winner.

Candy Graph

■ WHY DO IT?

To provide hands-on experiences with physical graphs

To learn to organize and record information

To learn to interpret physical (and pictorial) graphs

■ HERE'S HOW!

1. Provide the learners with a bar graph and a small bag of candy (such as M&Ms® or Skittles®).
2. Have the learners choose three colors of candy that they will graph and write the colors on the bar graph.
3. Have the learners take out only the three colors that they have chosen and physically place them on each appropriate square of the graph.

Red	Tan	Green

4. Then ask each learner questions about his or her graph. How many of each color did you get? Which color did you find the most of? The least? How many more green M&Ms did you find than red ones?
5. Finally, if appropriate, the learner may be allowed to eat the candy.

■ AN EASIER VARIATION:

1. Provide an egg carton and a small bag of candy (such as M&Ms or Skittles) for each learner.
2. Before opening the bag, have the learner choose two colors that he or she will graph.
3. Then use the egg carton as a graph by placing one piece of candy in each cup (and keeping the selected colors in line).
4. Ask the learner questions about his or her graph. Which color had the most? How many of that color did you find? Which color had the fewest?
5. Finally, the learner might then eat the candy.

■ AN ADVANCED VARIATION:

1. Provide the learners with a bar graph, crayons, and a small bag of candy (such as M&Ms or Skittles).
2. Have the learner choose three colors of candy that she will graph and write the colors on the bar graph.
3. Have the learner separate out the colors that she chose and use crayons of the same colors to mark in the corresponding squares of the graph.
4. Ask the learner to either eat the candy or put it away before asking questions about his or her graph. How many of each color did you get? What was your total? Which color did you find the most of? The least? How many more of one color M&Ms did you find than another? (*Note:* As such, the learner must interpret his or her findings from the pictorial graph rather than directly from the physical objects.)

People Graphs

WHY DO IT?

To collect, graph, and analyze data about people

HERE'S HOW!

1. Select a small group of people (family members or classmates) that the learners will graph in several ways.
2. The learners might first find out and graph the numbers that are girls and boys. (Grid paper for making graphs is found in Appendix A.)
3. Other graphs, for the same group of people, might consider eye color or hair color. Ask questions that compare the graphed information, such as: Are there more boys or girls? Do more of these people have blue or brown eyes? (Sample graphs are shown.)

7		
6		
5		
4		
3		
2		
1		
	Girls	Boys

7		
6		
5		
4		
3		
2		
1		
	Brown Eyes	Blue Eyes

7		
6		
5		
4		
3		
2		
1		
	Brown Hair	Blond Hair

AN EASIER VARIATION:

1. Make a floor tile graph by using masking tape to mark off two adjacent columns of square floor tiles (or use chalk to mark off a similar grid on a sidewalk).
2. Allow the learners to borrow one shoe from each of ten or more different pairs.
3. Have the learners make a shoe graph by placing all the shoes that have ties in one column and all the shoes without ties (slip ons, Velcro, buckles) in the other column.
4. Have the learners identify the type of shoe there is more of. How many more? How many fewer? How many shoes have been put on the entire graph? If we put the matching shoe with each of these to make a pair, how many shoes will we have all together?

AN ADVANCED VARIATION:

1. Have the learners ask at least 10 adults what their favorite leisure time activity is. They will likely find a wide range of activities from reading to fishing to playing music to playing tennis to going to the movies.
2. Ask the learners to graph the initial findings, but also to keep asking people and adding information to the graph for several days or even weeks.
3. When finished, ask what they discovered from the people graph?
4. As an extension, the learners might be asked how the adult leisure time activities might compare with those for kids? If an interest is expressed, a kids graph might also be developed.

Candy Estimate

▪ WHY DO IT?

To practice estimation and logical thinking

To group and count by tens and ones

▪ HERE'S HOW!

1. Provide 20 to 25 pieces of candy (jelly beans, M&Ms®, Skittles®, or gum drops) and a see-through container large enough to hold the candy.
2. Have Player #1 place an unknown amount of candy in the container.
3. Then each player must estimate (guess) whether there are more or less than 10 pieces in the container.
4. Another player should then take the candy from the container and match it on a 1-to-1 basis (one piece of candy to one dot) on 10 strip like the one shown.
5. Have the players count together to determine whether the actual amount of candy was greater than, less than, or exactly 10. (*Note:* For amounts greater than 10, encourage the players to begin at ten and count on as 10, 11, 12, 13, and 14.)

•	•	•	•	•	•	•	•	•	•	•	•	•	•
1	2	3	4	5	6	7	8	9	10	11	12	13	14

▪ AN EASIER VARIATION:

1. Provide small pieces of candy and a tablespoon.
2. Have the learner estimate (guess) how many pieces of candy could fit on the spoon.
3. Have the learner place candy on the spoon, one piece at a time, until a piece drops off.
4. Help the learner count the actual number of candies that were on the spoon before any dropped off.
5. Discuss with the learner whether he made an estimate that was *close* to the actual amount. (*Note:* Children sometimes think that their guess is *bad* if they are not exactly right. Stress the idea that when estimating we try for a *close* guess, and that the more estimation practice we have, the more often our estimates will be *close*.)

■ AN ADVANCED VARIATION:

1. Provide 100 or more small pieces of candy (or other small objects such as beans or marbles) and a see-through container large enough to hold the candy.
2. One player begins by placing an unknown amount of candy in the container.
3. Each player then estimates (guesses) how many pieces of candy are in the container.
4. Have the players take the candies out of the container and put them into piles of tens and ones.
5. Help them count by tens and then ones to find out how many pieces of candy were actually in the container.
6. Talk with the players about their methods for estimating. They might say things like, "I counted a group of 10 and then tried to see how many 10's were in the container," or "I can hold 20 of the candies in one hand so I figured out how many handfuls there might be."

Cereal Guess

◼ WHY DO IT?

To practice using groups of items when estimating

To develop logical thinking strategies

To practice counting by fives and tens

◼ HERE'S HOW!

1. Have the learners count dry cereal pieces (Cheerios®, Froot Loops®, Spoon Size Shredded Wheat®) into groups of five.
2. Have them estimate (guess) how many groups of five it will take to fill a small container (such as a custard cup or a juice glass).
3. Have the learner put cereal (in groups of five) into the container and count or tally the number of groups it took to fill it.
4. Talk about how close the learner's estimate was to the actual number of groups needed. When finished the learner may be allowed to eat the cereal.
5. As an extension, repeat the activity with groups of ten.

◼ AN EASIER VARIATION:

1. Estimate how many tablespoons of dry cereal (Cheerios, Froot Loops, Spoon Size Shredded Wheat) will be needed to fill a small container.
2. Have the learner count the number of tablespoons of cereal it takes to fill the container.
3. Talk about whether or not the estimate was close to the actual count.

◼ AN ADVANCED VARIATION:

1. Have the learner count how many tablespoons of dry cereal (Cheerios, Froot Loops, Spoon Size Shredded Wheat) are needed to fill a cereal bowl.
2. Next, ask the learner to count the number of cereal pieces it takes to fill one tablespoon.
3. Then have the learner estimate how many pieces of cereal are in the bowl.
4. On a paper towel or waxed paper, have the learner take the cereal pieces from the bowl and organize them in groups of 10. Ask how many groups of 10 she found? Have the learner count by 10s (and/or 100s, if necessary) to find the total.
5. Talk about how close her estimate was to the actual total. If off by a lot, is there a way she might have achieved a closer answer?

A Pocket Full of Change

■ WHY DO IT?

To recognize pennies, nickels, dimes, and quarters
To become familiar with the monetary value of coins

■ HERE'S HOW!

1. Provide a pocket full of change.
2. Have the learners sort the coins into pennies, nickels, dimes, and quarters and count the number of each type.
3. Help the learners to find out how much money value is represented in each group. The pennies can be counted 1 to 1. Then, if the learner is capable, the nickels should be counted by 5s as 5¢, 10¢, 15¢, and so forth; the dimes by 10s as 10¢, 20¢, 30¢, and so forth. Finally, if not too difficult, help the learners to count all of the coins to determine the total value of the pocket full of money.
4. If a further *challenge* is desired, the coins might be divided randomly in half and two players assigned to sort the two group of coins. The players should determine who has the most pennies, nickels, dimes, and quarters. They might also find and compare the total money value of each half. (*Note:* The largest number of coins does not necessarily represent the greatest total monetary value.)

■ AN EASIER VARIATION:

1. Locate the book *26 Letters And 99 Cents,* by Tana Hoban.[1]
2. Have the learners use actual coins and match them with the coins pictured in the book.
3. The learners should also note the numerals beside the pictures. These numerals represent the number of pennies and also the value of the money shown.
4. Help the learners to note, that beginning with the number 5, the different ways coins can be combined to make a specific amount of money.
5. As a special *challenge,* for the child who has a good grasp of money and coin combinations, begin with the number 11 and ask how many combinations, in addition to those shown in the book, will equal the values shown. (For example, with 11 one dime and one penny are displayed, but also shown might be two nickels and a penny, one nickel and six pennies, or 11 pennies.)

◼ AN ADVANCED VARIATION:

1. Provide a restaurant menu (a children's menu if possible) that lists food items and their costs.
2. Help the learners to translate the cost of each item into an equivalent amount in coins. A hamburger that costs 98 cents, for example, might be paid for with 3 quarters, two dimes, and 3 pennies. (*Note:* Learners, comfortable with the related concepts, might also use dollar bills.
3. As a further *challenge* students might compare the total for individual purchases at a fast food restaurant versus the cost of the same items bought as a Value Meal.

I Predict!

◼ WHY DO IT?

To collect, organize, and interpret information

To introduce probability concepts

To enhance logical thinking skills

◼ HERE'S HOW!

1. Use socks of two different colors.
2. Player #1 begins by secretly putting a number of socks of each color into a paper bag.
3. Player #2 reaches into the bag, pulls out one of the socks, and then replaces it. He may continue to pull out and replace socks from the bag, one at a time, as many times as desired.
4. When Player #2 thinks he knows which color represents the largest number of socks in the bag, he guesses that color.
5. Take out and display the socks to determine which color actually represents the largest number and talk about any difference.
6. As an extension, use socks of three or four different colors when doing the activity.

◼ AN EASIER VARIATION:

1. Provide five dimes and five pennies. Have the learner look at them and count each set of coins.
2. Place all of the coins in a paper bag.
3. Allow the learner to shake the bag, predict which coin she will pull out, and, without looking, select a coin.
4. Keep track of each prediction and each coin selected.
5. After several attempts have the learner tell how often the coin predicted was correct and why she was not correct every time.
6. Next, remove the five dimes and redo the activity.
7. There will be an increase in the number of correct predictions. Ask the child to explain why she can now predict correctly every time.

◼ AN ADVANCED VARIATION:

1. Cut 1 inch squares from three different colors of paper. Secretly place 10 squares (three of one color, three of another color, and four of a third color) into a paper bag.
2. Have the learner shake the bag, pull out one square without looking, record the color on a tally sheet, and put the square back into the bag.

	TALLY MARKS	HOW MANY
RED	/////	5
BLUE	///	3
YELLOW	//	2

3. Have the learner shake the bag and repeat the process ten times.
4. Then ask the learner to predict how many squares of each color are in the bag and why he thinks so. Also ask, "If your first guess isn't quite correct, what is your next best guess as to how many squares of each color are in the bag?"
5. After predictions have been made, allow the learner to empty the bag, count the actual number of each color, compare it with his tally marks, and talk about *how close* he was and why.
6. As an extension, repeat the activity using different numbers of each color. When finished, talk about the results and how they compare with his predictions.

Peek Boxes

■ WHY DO IT?

To provide experiences collecting, organizing, and interpreting data

To learn about making probable (probability) guesses

To develop logical thinking abilities

■ HERE'S HOW!

1. Provide a small box with one corner cut off and marbles of two different colors. When the learners aren't looking put 10 marbles in the box (such as 2 green and 8 yellow).

2. Tell the learner that the box contains 10 marbles and that there are both green and yellow marbles. She may then shake the box several times (perhaps 10), peek at the corner each time, and make a guess as to how many are probably green and how many are probably yellow.

3. Talk with the learner about *why* she thought there were a certain number of each color.

4. Have the learner try the peek box experiment several more times and keep records for each trial (perhaps by making a tally mark each time a certain color appears).

5. Does she still think the first answer was best? Why or why not? (*Note:* The top may be opened so that the learner might examine the actual number of marbles of each color.)

6. Try the peek box activity again, but use a different number of marbles of each color.

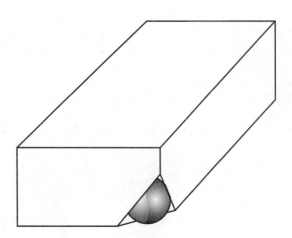

AN EASIER VARIATION:

1. Provide a peek box that contains 3 green marbles and 3 yellow marbles.
2. Allow the learner to shake and peek several times. Then ask what color the marbles are in the peek box? If there are 6 marbles in the peek box, how many do you think there are of each color?
3. Try the activity again with 1 green marble and 5 yellow marbles. If the learner has seen only yellow marbles, ask if there could be any green marbles? (*Note:* The box may be opened and looked into.)

AN ADVANCED VARIATION:

1. If the learners appear ready, try peek boxes with more marbles (perhaps 20), but only allow 10 shakes. After he has completed the 10 shakes and tallies, ask what the probable (probability) total number of marbles of each color is?
2. Allow the learners several more trials. Then ask them to compare their findings and answer the following statement. "I think there are _____ green marbles and _____ yellow marbles in the peek box, but there could be _____ green marbles and _____ yellow marbles because _____ .

My Lucky Number

◼ WHY DO IT?

To gain experience with probability (probable) outcomes

To develop logical thinking skills

To practice addition to 12

◼ HERE'S HOW!

1. Provide two dice, pencils or crayons of different colors, and a chart like the one shown.
2. Allow each player to pick a *Lucky Number* (from 2 to 12) and circle it with his or her special color.
3. Have the players take turns rolling the dice and adding up the dots.
4. At each turn put a tally mark under each total number that is rolled. (If 2 and 4 are rolled, put a tally mark under the number 6).
5. The first person to get 5 tally marks under his or her *Lucky Number* wins.
6. Pick another *Lucky Number* and play again. After playing several times ask the learners if they can make a better guess as to which numbers have more chances of winning?

	2	3	4	5	6	7	8	9	10	11	12
Game 1											
Game 2											
Game 3											
Game 4											

AN EASIER VARIATION:

1. Provide two dice that have the numbers 1, 2, 3, 1, 2, 3 on them. (See Appendix A for directions on how to make or modify dice.)
2. Help the learner to make a chart, but with the numbers 2 through 6 across the top.
3. Then play the game as described above (with the new dice and numbers) and, after several games, talk about the outcomes.

AN ADVANCED VARIATION:

1. Obtain two 1 through 6 dice and label them **Die 1** and **Die 2.**
2. Have the learners roll the two dice and plot the sums of the rolls on the chart. How many different ways can the sums 2 through 12 be obtained.
3. Read the chart to determine how many different ways you can achieve each sum (1 through 12). Write the answers on the appropriate lines in the list below.

There are _____ ways to get 1.

There are _____ ways to get 2.

There are _____ ways to get 3.

There are _____ ways to get 4.

There are _____ ways to get 5.

There are _____ ways to get 6.

There are _____ ways to get 7.

There are _____ ways to get 8.

There are _____ ways to get 9.

There are _____ ways to get 10.

There are _____ ways to get 11.

There are _____ ways to get 12.

Die #1 * * Die #2	1	2	3	4	5	6
1						
2						
3						
4						
5						
6						

Colorful "Squiggle" Designs

■ WHY DO IT?

To enhance logical thinking and problem-solving skills
To enjoy making predictions and developing strategies
To develop mapping skills

■ HERE'S HOW!

1. Have the learner draw a simple "squiggle" design (see example) by placing a pencil anywhere on a sheet of paper and drawing a line, without lifting the pencil, that repeatedly crosses over itself and ends at the starting point.
2. Next, select markers or crayons of two different hues and, adhering to the following rule, color in the segments of the design. (*Rule:* Segments of the same color may not share a common boundary line [edge]. Segments of the same color may touch only at a vertex.)
3. If playing with a partner, take turns coloring segments and follow the rule noted above.

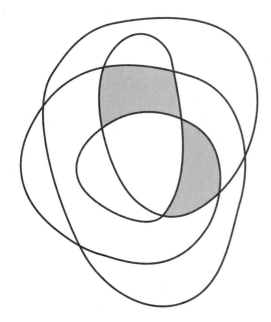

This is allowed

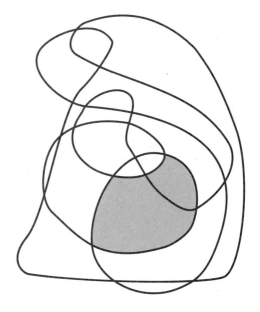

This is NOT allowed

4. Have the learners notice and talk about whether it was possible to color in all sections of the "squiggle" design.
5. To extend the experience, have the learners draw another design and color it following the same rule. Is it possible to color every section? Why or why not?

■ AN EASIER VARIATION:

1. Have the learner use a dark crayon to draw a "squiggle" design (see example).
2. She should then shade in the individual segments with different colors to create a colorful design.
3. Talk about the design. Count the total number of segments. How many segments of each color did she make? Does the design look like something special?
4. If a *challenge* is desired, ask the learner to draw another "squiggle" design and shade it in with just two colors according to the following rule. (*Rule:* Segments of the same color may not touch at an edge. They may however touch at a single point [vertex].) When she has finished, ask what she found out?

■ AN ADVANCED VARIATION:

1. Photocopy the provided "squiggle" design (see example) and have the learners predict the fewest number of colors needed to color the design if sections of the same color cannot share a common boundary (edge), but can touch at a vertex. Have the learners try it and talk about the outcome.
2. Have the learners draw another "squiggle" design, but this time do not have them stop the line at the starting point. Instead allow it to roam the page until they find a stopping point that closes a segment. Predict the fewest number of colors needed to color this design (no two sections of the same color may share a common boundary). Try it to find out. Were their predictions correct? What accounts for the results?
3. If a further *challenge* is desired, have the learners use a pencil and a straight edge to section a paper into boxlike segments. Predict how many colors it will take to fill in all of these segments so that no two segments of the same color share a common boundary. Talk about the results of this *new* experiment.

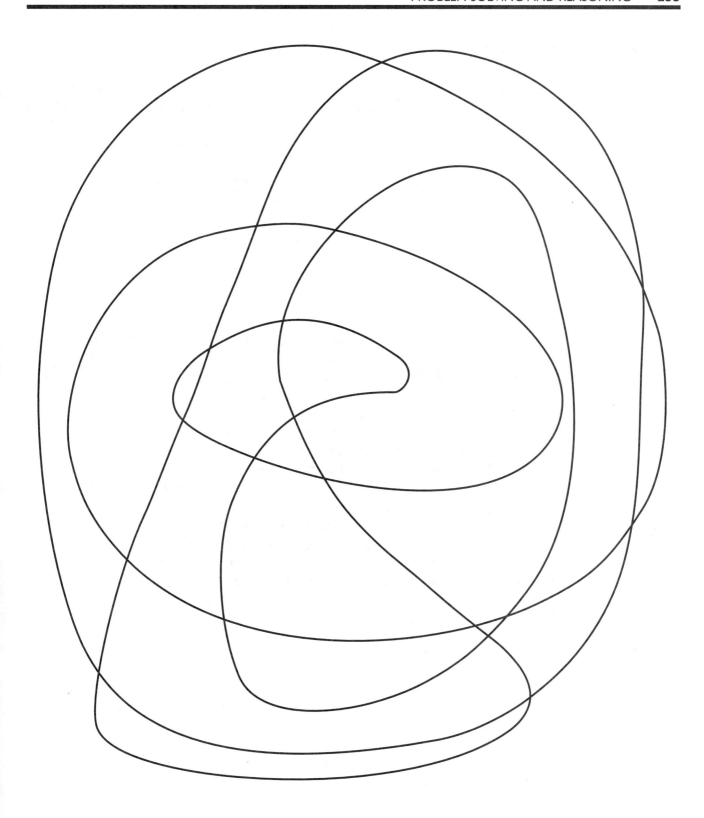

Build a Network

■ WHY DO IT?

To introduce learners to mathematical networks
To develop game strategies and problem-solving skills

■ HERE'S HOW!

1. Photocopy the *Smiley Face Game Board* (on the next page) and provide a coin and a pencil for each two players.
2. The players take turns flipping the coin and drawing lines between dots. If, for example, Player #1 flips a tail, he must draw a line on the game board that is 1 space long and connects two dots either horizontally or vertically. Player #2 might then flip a head and be allowed to draw a 2 space line or two 1 space lines. (*Note:* heads = 2 spaces and tails = 1 space.)
3. When a player is able to draw a line that encloses a square, that player gets to write his or her initials in the box.
4. When all dots have been connected, the players count the squares with their initials to determine their scores. (*Note:* Plain squares are worth one point and smiley face squares are worth two points.)

■ AN EASIER VARIATION:

1. Provide a sheet of paper with 10 to 20 dots marked randomly across it.
2. The learner should then create a network by drawing straight lines from dot to dot (see example).
3. The child may then color in the areas of the network to make a design.

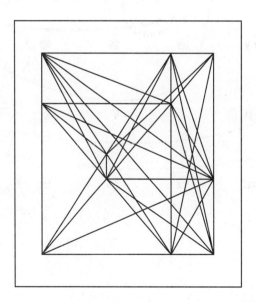

PUT ON A SMILEY FACE GAME BOARD

◼ AN ADVANCED VARIATION:

1. Read the story *Rosie's Walk*[2] by Pat Hutchins.
2. Have the learners talk about the directional words and the fact that Rosie doesn't know the fox is following her.
3. Play a game where Rosie learns about the fox and plans a strategy for staying out of his way as she takes her daily walk through the barnyard. The fox is, however, planning ways to catch her. Can Rosie find a route back to the hen house and avoid meeting the sneaky fox?
4. Use *Rosie's Barnyard Walk* Game Board and markers representing Rosie and the fox.
5. Two players flip a coin at each turn to see how many moves they can make. (Heads = two moves; tails = one move.)
6. Players may start at any star point on the outside boundary of the game board and move in any direction along the network paths.
7. Play continues until the Rosie reaches the Hen House or the fox catches her.

ROSIE'S BARNYARD WALK

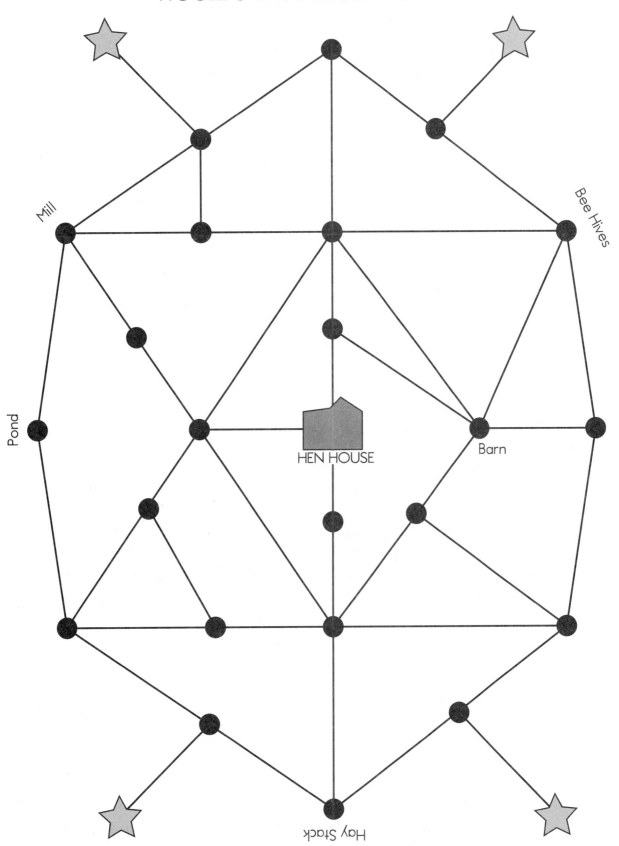

Works Cited

1. Tana Hoban, *26 Letters and 99 Cents* (New York: Greenwillow Books division of William Morrow and Company, 1988).
2. Pat Hutchins, *Rosie's Walk* (New York: Collier Books/Macmillan, 1968).

Appendixes

The items in these Appendixes, in addition to those found within the text, are provided in order that children might more easily understand and/or extend their mathematical understandings. Provided first are simple learning aids and devices that can be used directly by young learners. Next are books and computer software that will help to enhance and extend children's' mathematical understandings. Finally, a listing of selected sources for use by parents and/or teachers is provided.

Appendix A: Simple Equipment to Make or Acquire

Appendix B: Selected Resources for Use with Young Children

239

Appendix C: Selected Sources for Parents and Teachers

Appendix D: Recommended Developmental Experiences

Appendix A: Simple Equipment to Make or Acquire

MAKE A PAPER CLIP SPINNER:

1. Lay a paper clip so that one end overlaps the center point of the spinner chart.

2. Put a pencil point through the end loop of the paper clip and hold it on the center point of the chart.

3. Use your other hand to spin the paper clip. The paper clip will point to different numbers at random.

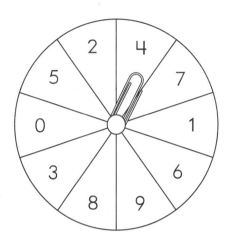

CONSTRUCTING MILK CARTON DICE:

1. Obtain and thoroughly clean two milk cartons.

2. Cut off the bottom portions of the cartons at a height ¼ inch less than the width of the cartons.

3. Form a cube by pushing the open end of one milk carton into the open end of the other.

4. Cover the cube with Contac® paper.

5. Use a Magic Marker® or stick-on labels to put any desired images (dots, numerals, geometric shapes, fractions, and so forth) on the faces of each cube.

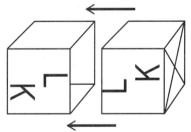

MODIFYING REGULAR DICE:

1. Use standard dot dice or any cubes will work.

2. Obtain small glue-backed stick-on labels from an office supply or stationary store.

3. Pen or pencil any desired images on the labels and stick them onto the faces of each die. You may want some that show numerals as 1, 2, 3, 4, 5, and 6; or limit the range of numbers to 1, 2, 3 and 1, 2, 3 again; or show a fractional part shaded in; or geometric shapes, and so forth.

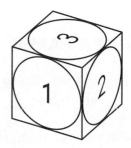
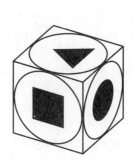

EASY FINGER PAINT:

1. Dampen art paper with a wet sponge.
2. Pour 2 or 3 tablespoons of liquid starch onto the paper.
3. Sprinkle $1/2$ teaspoon of tempera paint onto the liquid.
4. Use the learner's fingers to mix the color in and paint.
5. Extend the learner's experience by sprinkling 2 colors at a time (such as yellow and blue or red and yellow) onto the paper; the learner will discover a third color.

COOKED FINGER PAINT:

$1/2$ cup dry starch   vegetable coloring

$1^1/3$ cups boiling water   1 tsp. glycerin

$1/2$ cup soap flakes

1. Mix the starch with enough cold water to make a smooth paste.
2. Add boiling water and cook the paste until glossy.
3. Stir in the dry soap flakes while the mixture is still warm.
4. Allow the mixture to cool.
5. Add glycerin and pour the mixture into jars.
6. Add color later when ready to use.
7. The mixture can be kept for a week if it is tightly covered.

EASY PLAY DOUGH:

3 cups flour

³/₄ cup salt

¹/₂ cup water

liquid tempera paint or 2 tsp. food coloring (optional)

1. Sift flour and salt together into a pan.
2. Mix coloring with water and add gradually to flour and salt mixture.
3. Knead until the mixture is smooth and easy to handle.
4. If mixture becomes sticky, add more flour.
5. When not in use, place in a plastic bag and keep in a cool place.
6. Easy Play Dough will last at least two weeks.

COOKED (HARDENING) PLAY DOUGH:

1 cup flour

1 tablespoon oil

1 cup water

¹/₂ cup salt

2 teaspoons cream of tartar

food coloring or tempera paint

1. Combine all ingredients in a sauce pan.
2. Cook over medium heat.
3. Stir constantly until mixture forms a ball.
4. Knead until smooth.
5. Store in a covered container.

AN INCH RULER:

1	2	3	4	5	6
					INCHES

A CENTIMETER RULER:

1	2	3	4	5	6	7	8	9	10	11	12	13	14	15
														cm

TO CONSTRUCT A PAPER THERMOMETER:

Photocopy the demonstration paper thermometer (below) and help the learner cut it out and glue it onto a piece of cardboard. Carefully cut slits on the dotted lines. Also cut out the two thin paper strips and color one red (or use colored paper) and glue the A and B ends together. Thread the paper strips through the slits so that the ends are on the back side and the red portion is at the bottom of the thermometer. Ask the learner to show a particular temperature by pulling the strips up or down so the red line matches the appropriate temperature number.

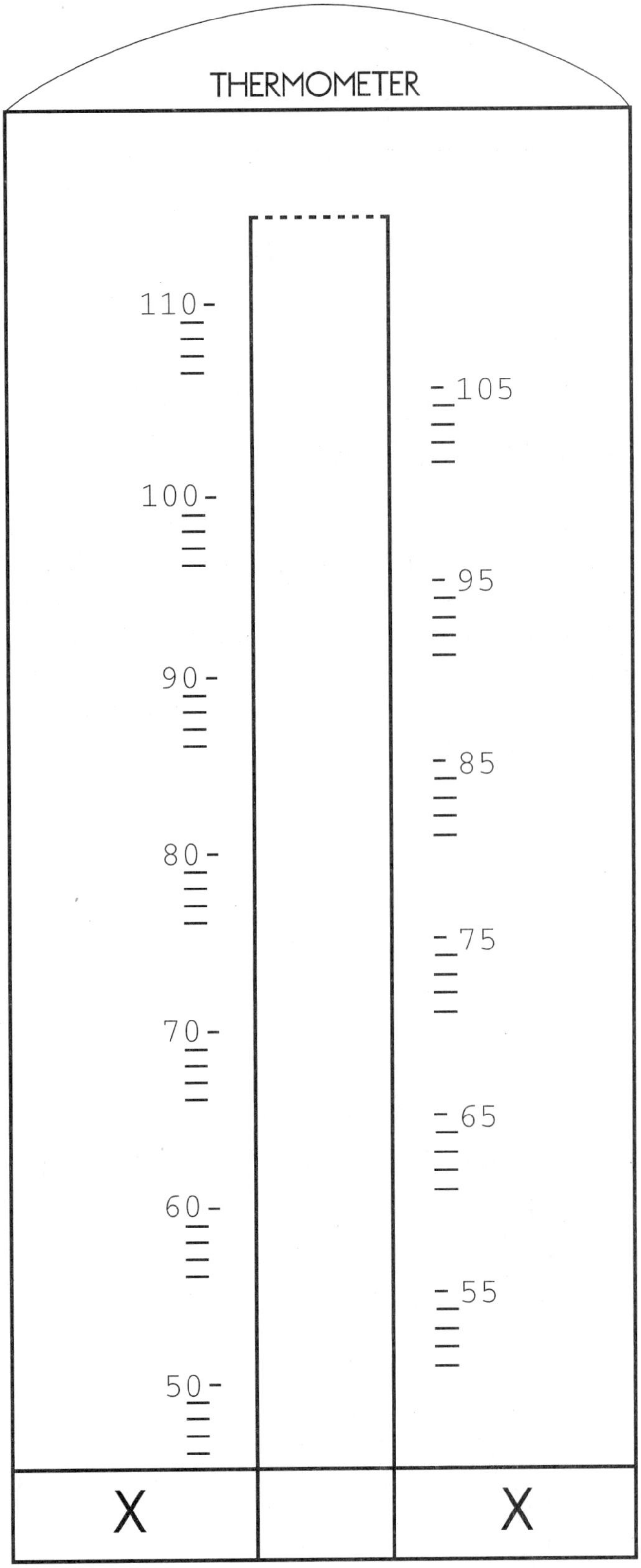

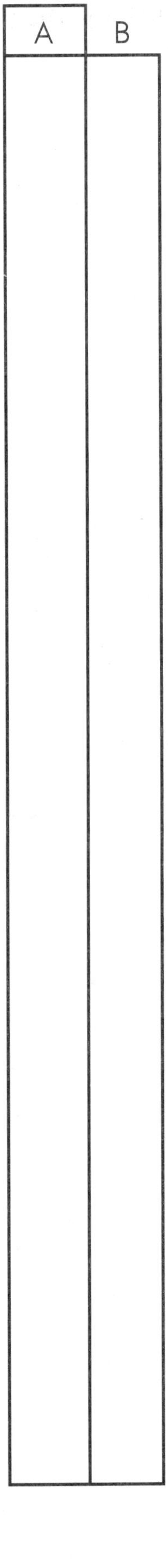

THERMOMETER

110–
100–
90–
80–
70–
60–
50–

- 105
- 95
- 85
- 75
- 65
- 55

X

X

A   B

Trim this section and paste over x's

```
                            - 45
                            =

        40 -
           =
                            - 35
                            =
        30 -
           =
                            - 25
                            =
        20 -
           =
                            - 15
                            =
        10 -
           =
                            - 5
                            =
         0 -
           =
                            - -5
                            =
       -10 -
           =
```

INCH GRAPH PAPER:

HALF-INCH GRAPH PAPER:

CENTIMETER GRAPH PAPER:

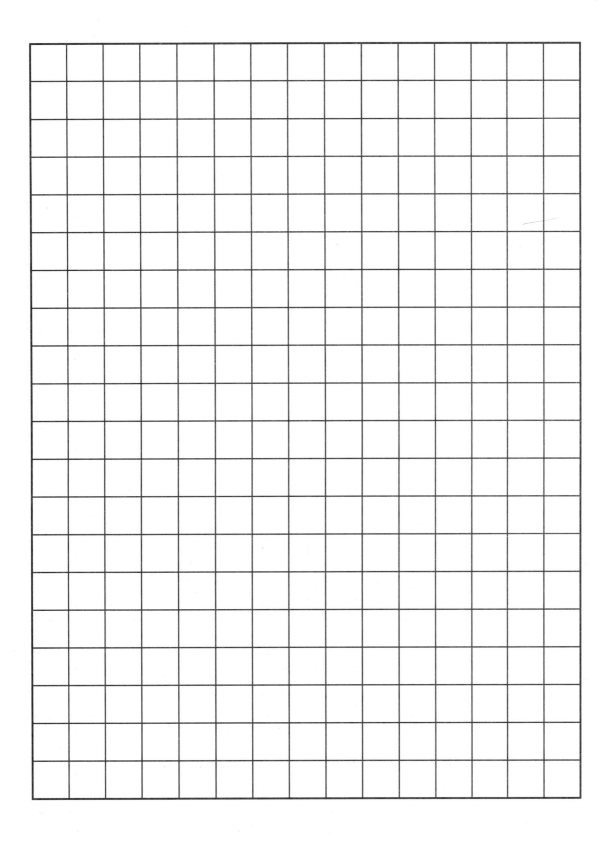

DOT PAPER:

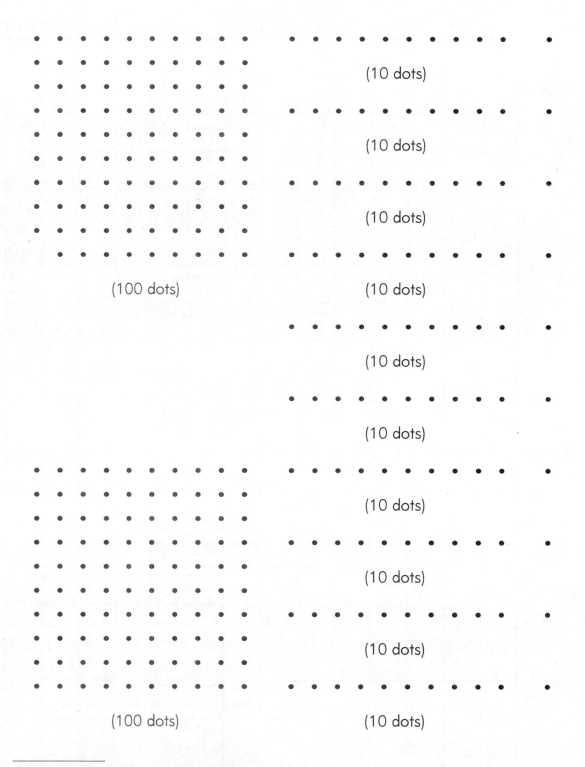

(10 dots)

(10 dots)

(10 dots)

(100 dots)   (10 dots)

(10 dots)

(10 dots)

(10 dots)

(10 dots)

(100 dots)   (10 dots)

(*Note:* Use the single dots when counting to 10. Each time 10 dots are collected, trade them in for a 10-dot strip; then, if the child is capable, count by 10s to 100 and trade for a group of 100 dots, and so forth.)

Appendix B: Selected Resources for Use with Young Children

Books:

Children need to experience math in a variety of ways in order to understand the concepts and how they connect to the real world. Children's books can be used to help teach mathematical concepts in a variety of ways. Some books have an obvious focus on math and help teach a specific concept; others can be used to encourage mathematical investigations and concept exploration. There are also books that have no obvious math connections, but that can be used to enhance the child's critical thinking and investigative skills

Below is a selected list of children's literature books with a brief description of each. The books are listed alphabetically by author and correlated with the appropriate chapter headings in *Big Math Activities for Young Children*. (A notation follows each book that was used as part of an activity within this text.)

This list represents only a few of the books that might be used to introduce math to young children. New books are published on a regular basis. Check your public library and local book stores for additional books that can be used to broaden math concept learning and enhance literacy in general.

Number Sense and Counting (Chapter 1):

Allison, Linda. *Eenie, Meenie, Miney Math: Math for You and Your Preschooler.* Boston: Little, Brown, 1993.
This book, written especially for parents, is a collection of quick playful activities and games to introduce math to young children. The activities can be done anytime and anywhere as children look at and learn about colors, shapes, patterns, numbers, and counting.

Anno, Mitsumasa. *Anno's Counting Book.* New York: Harper & Row, 1977.
One year in the life of a small village. The illustrations show many things to count.

Bang, Molly. *Ten, Nine, Eight.* New York: Greenwillow Books/William Morrow, 1983.
A young girl falls asleep as her mother counts from 10 to 1 in a lullaby.

Carle, Eric. *My Very First Book of Numbers.* New York: Harper & Row, 1974.
A counting book with split pages. Groups of objects appear on the top half and can be matched by turning the bottom half of the page to find the corresponding number.

Crews, Donald. *Ten Black Dots.* New York: Greenwillow Books/ William Morrow, 1968.
What can you do with ten dots? One dot makes a sun or a moon when the day is done. Simple rhymes and everyday objects are used to count to 10.

Dee, Ruby. *Two Ways to Count to Ten*. New York: Henry Holt and Co., 1988.
  A retold traditional tale that shows the cleverness of one animal who wins the prize by counting by 2's.

Ehlert, Lois. *Fish Eyes, A Book You Can Count On*. San Diego, CA: Harcourt, Brace & Jovanovich, 1990.
  Children enjoy learning to count brilliantly colored fish swimming through the pages. A friendly guide joins in the journey and helps out with simple addition.

Enderle, Judith, and Stephanie Tessler. *Where Are You Little Zack?* New York: Houghton Mifflin, 1997.
  The four duck brothers take the number one train on track two to the city but when they get there, little Zack is missing. An amusing story of how they count their way to finding brother Zack.

Falwell, Cathryn. *Feast for 10*. New York: Clarion Books/Houghton Mifflin, 1993.
  A family of four shops and prepares a feast for ten.

Hamm, Diane Johnston. *How Many Feet in the Bed?* New York: Simon & Schuster, 1991.
  A family of five gets in and out of bed on a Sunday morning. This story presents many ways to count by twos.

Hargreaves, Roger. *Count Worm*. Miami, FL: P.S.I. & Associates, Ottenheimer Publishers, 1982.
  A friendly and very agile worm helps a young boy learn to count and recognize the shape of each number. (Number Bake: Easier Variation)

McGrath, Barbara Barbieri. *The M&M Counting Book,* Watertown, WA: Charlesbridge Publishing, 1994.
  This yummy counting book teaches numbers 1 through 12, six colors, and three primary shapes. Lucky learners are rewarded when they learn simple subtraction by eating the problem.

Sloat, Teri. *From One to One Hundred*. New York: Dutton Children's Books/Penguin Books, 1991.
  A picture book with no text. Children search the illustrations to find the numbers.

Number Operations (Chapter 2):

Anno, Mitsumasi. *Anno's Mysterious Multiplying Jar*. New York: Philomel, 1983.
  The story teaches multiplication through illustrations as objects are revealed in Mr. Anno's jar.

Christelow, Eileen. *Five Little Monkeys Jumping on the Bed*. New York: Clarion Books/Houghton Mifflin, 1989.
  Subtraction and addition can be illustrated by this amusing familiar rhyme.

Hoban, Tana. *26 Letters and 99 Cents*. New York: Scholastic/William Morrow, 1987.
  Letters are introduced with pictures of related items. Photos of coins are shown to illustrate numbers. A penny represents the number 1. As the numbers get larger, a variety of coins are shown to represent the number 5, the number 11, and so forth. (Money Match Math, Alternate Variation)

Hutchins, Pat. *The Doorbell Rang*. New York: William Morrow, 1986.
>   In this story, a dozen cookies are shared with an ever-changing number of children. Each time the cookies are redistributed to give each child an equal number. A surprise ending saves the day! (Table Math: More Difficult Variation)

Long, Lynette. *Domino Addition*. Watertown, WA: Charlesbridge Publishing, 1996.
>   This book takes the traditional game of dominos and gives it an entirely new use. Games and challenges are given to players as they practice different operations.

Viorst, Judith. *Alexander, Who Used to Be Rich Last Sunday*. New York: Atheneum, 1979.
>   Alexander is given a dollar bill by his grandparents. He buys items of questionable quality until his money dwindles little by little. (What Price, More Advanced Variation)

Measurement (Chapter 3):

Carlstrom, Nancy. *Jesse Bear, What Will You Wear?* New York: Macmillan, 1986.
>   Jesse Bear goes through the day deciding what to wear in various situations.

Carlstrom, Nancy. *It's About Time Jesse Bear and Other Rhymes*. New York: Macmillan, 1990.
>   This cheerful story, told in rhyme, follows the little bear through the day as he learns about time. (It's Time, Easier Variation)

McMillan, Bruce. *Eating Fractions*. New York: Scholastic, 1991.
>   Two children share a tasty meal by dividing various foods. It shows fractions as parts of a whole using units of halves, thirds, and fourths.

Schwartz, David. *If You Made a Million*. New York: Mulberry Books, William Morrow, 1989.
>   Written in child language and around children's interest areas, this book talks about what a million is; how to make a million and what to do with it after you have it. Making and spending money means making choices.

Williams, Vera. *A Chair for My Mother*. New York: Greenwillow Books/William Morrow, 1982.
>   After a fire destroys their possessions, a family saves their money to buy a new chair.

Geometry (Chapter 4):

Baker, Alan. *Brown Rabbit's Shape Book*. New York: Larousse, Kingfisher & Cambers, 1994.
>   Brown Rabbit receives a mysterious package. He looks through the various shaped containers until he discovers what is inside.

Carle, Eric. *My First Book of Shapes*. New York: Thomas Crowell, 1994.
>   Geometric shapes are shown and children are asked to associate them with everyday items.

Grover, Max. *Circles and Squares Everywhere*. San Diego, CA: Browndeer Press/ Harcourt, Brace, 1996.
> Welcome to the world of circles and squares. This picture book shows the use of these shapes in tires, trucks, windows, smokestacks, and boats. Max says, "There are circles and squares everywhere!"

Hoban, Tana. *Circles, Triangles, and Squares*. New York: Macmillan, 1974.
> A study of geometric shapes in the world around us.

Hoban, Tana. *Round and Round and Round*. New York: Greenwillow Books division of William Morrow and Company, 1988.
> This book, with no written text, is a series of silhouettes arranged in groups. Children identify the items and tell what they have in common.

Problem Solving and Reasoning (Chapter 5):

Anno, Mitsumasa. *Anno's Math Games*. New York: Philomel Books, 1991.
> Games and math challenges for a range of ages and abilities.

Aruego, Jose, and Ariane Dewey. *We Hide, You Seek*. New York: Greenwillow Books/ William Morrow, 1997.
> A clumsy rhino is talked into a game of hide and seek. His clumsiness allows him to startle the animals into revealing themselves from their camouflaged hiding places.

Hoban, Tana. *26 Letters and 99 Cents*. New York: Greenwillow Books division of William Morrow and Company, 1987. (Pocketful of Change, Easier Variation see Chapter 2 listing.)

Hutchins, Pat. *Rosie's Walk*. New York: Macmillan, 1968.
> Rosie the hen goes for a walk. As she strolls through the barnyard, she is unaware of a fox following her. She has several narrow escapes, but the fox isn't so lucky! (Build a Network: Advanced Variation)

Leighton, Ralph, and Carl Feyman, *How To Count Sheep Without Falling Asleep*. New York: Prentice Hall, 1976.
> This book teaches the history of numbers through entertaining illustrations. It suggests that the need for numbers arose because caveman needed a way to count their sheep.

Oaks, Bill, and Suse MacDonald. *Puzzlers*. New York: Dial Books for Young Readers/ Penguin Books, 1989.
> A book filled with special animals that are made up of numbers. The numbers are bulging wide, stretching tall, tumbling down, and lined up back to back. How many numbers can you find?

Reid, Margaret. *The Button Box*. New York: Dutton Children's Books/Penguin Books, 1990.
> A child who loves to play with his grandmother's box of buttons sorts them into groups based on their attributes.

Computer Software:

Countdown from Voyager, 578 Broadway, Suite 406, New York, NY 10012, (212) 431–5199 (Mac/Windows)

Early Math (for ages 3–6) from Bright Star Technology, Inc./Sierra On-line, Inc., P.O. Box 53250, Bellevue, WA 98015–3250 (Mac/Windows)

Kid Pix from Broderbund, P.O. Box 6125, Novato, CA 94948–6125, (800) 474–8840 (Mac/Windows)

Mathosaurus (grades K, 1 & 2) from Micrograms Software, 1404 N. Main Street, Rockford, IL 61103, (800) 338–4726 (Mac/Windows)

Millie's Math House (ages 2–5) from Edmark, 6727 185th Ave. NE, Redmond, WA 98073–3218, (800) 691–2985 (Mac/Windows)

Treasure Math Storm (ages 5–9) from The Learning Company, 1 Athenaeum Street, Cambridge, MA 02142, (800) 852–2255 (Mac/Windows)

Trudy's Time and Place House (for ages 3–6) from Edmark, 6727 185th Ave. NE, Redmond, WA 98073–3218, (800) 691–2985 (Mac/Windows)

Appendix C: Selected Sources for Parents and Teachers

Books:

Baratta-Lorton, Mary. *Workjobs for Parents*. Menlo Park, CA: Addison-Wesley, 1975 (ISBN 0–201–04303–3).

Charlesworth, Rosalind. *Experiences in Math for Young Children,* Third Edition. Albany, NY: Delmar Publishers, 1996 (ISBN 0–8273–7226–4).

Foster, David, and James Overholt. *Indoor Action Games for Elementary Children*. Englewood Cliffs, NJ: Parker Publishing/Prentice Hall, 1989 (ISBN 0–13–459124–0).

Gestwicki, Carol. *The Essentials of Early Education*. Albany, NY: Delmar Publishers, 1997 (ISBN 0–8273–7282–5).

Overholt, James. *Math Wise: Hands-on Activities and Investigations for Elementary Students*. Englewood Cliffs, NJ: Center for Applied Research in Education/Prentice Hall, 1995 (ISBN 0–87628–555–8).

Magazines:

Association for Childhood Education International. *Childhood Education: Infancy through Early Adolescence* (6 issues per year). 17904 Georgia Avenue #215, Olney, MD 20832 (ISSN 0009–4056).

National Association for the Education of Young Children. *Young Children* (8 issues per year). 1509 16th Street, Washington, D.C. 20036–1426 (ISSN 0044–0728).

National Council of Teachers of Mathematics. *Teaching Children Mathematics* (8 issues per year). 1906 Association Drive, Reston, VA 20191–1593 (ISSN 1073–5836).

Scholastic, Inc. *Early Childhood Today* (8 issues per year). 2931 McCarthy St., P.O. Box 3710, Jefferson City, MO 65102–3710 (ISSN 1070–1214).

Video Tapes:

National Council of Teachers of Mathematics. *Reaching Higher: A Problem Solving Approach to Elementary School Mathematics* (Video). 1906 Association Drive, Reston, VA 20191 (ISBN 0–87353–304–6).

Richardson, Kathy. *A Look at Children's Thinking—Beginning Number Concepts* (Video I) and *Number Combinations and Place Value* (Video II). Educational Enrichment, Inc., P.O. Box 1524, 770 W. Rock Creek Rd., Norman, OK 73070.

Wilmot, Barbara. *Making Math Meaningful* (Videos I–IV). Meridian Education Corporation, 236 E. Front Street, Bloomington, IL 61701 (ISBN 1–56191–173–9).

Internet Sites:

HELPING YOUR CHILD LEARN MATH (activities for ages 5 through 13)
<http://www.ed.gov/pubs/parents/Math/index.html>

LET'S DO MATH!
<http://www.ed.gov/pubs/parents/LearnPtnrs/math.html>

ROAD MAP TO THE WORLD WIDE WEB (Mathematics)
<http://www.thejournal.com/roadmap/math.html>

THE MATH FORUM
<http://forum.swarthmore.edu/>

ERIC CLEARINGHOUSE ON EARLY CHILDHOOD & ELEMENTARY EDUCATION
<http://ericps.crc.uiuc.edu/ericeece.html>

FUN & USEFUL SITES FOR KIDS
<http://forum.swarthmore.edu/~steve/steve/edkids.html>

SCORE MATHEMATICS (K–4 Resources)
<http://www.kings.k12.ca.us/math/k.4.html>

WHAT SHOULD BE LEARNED IN KINDERGARTEN?
<http://www.aspensys.com/eric/kinderga.html>

A GUIDE TO HELPING YOUR CHILD UNDERSTAND MATHEMATICS
<http://www.eduplace.com/math/res/parentbk/index.html>

HELPING YOUR CHILD REACH THE NEW STANDARDS IN MATHEMATICS, SCIENCE, AND TECHNOLOGY
<http://dimacs.rutgers.edu/nj_math_coalition/pguide/pguide.html>

TEACHERS HELPING TEACHERS
<http://www.pacificnet.net/~mandel/index.html>

MEGA MATHEMATICS
<http://www.cs.uidaho.edu/~casey931/mega-math/>

THE COUNTING GAME
<http://home.earthlink.net/~cmalumphy/countinggame.html>

NATURAL MATH: Book-on-the-Web
<http://www.naturalmath.com/>

NATIONAL ASSOCIATION FOR THE EDUCATION OF YOUNG CHILDREN
<http://www.naeyc.org/>

DELMAR PUBLISHERS: Early Childhood, Elementary & Special Education
<http://www.delmar.com/catalog/educate_index.html>

Appendix D: Recommended Developmental Experiences

Young children acquire math concepts and skills in stages. They gain understanding over time and at varying rates. They benefit from manipulating materials and exploring situations in a variety of ways. For example, early number skills, such as learning phone numbers and addresses, begin in the preschool years and help to prepare children for more complex mathematical skills such as addition and subtraction.

Informal math experiences occur daily in the world of young children. As they interact with a variety of materials and situations, children begin to understand the world around them and its relationship to mathematics. Parents and teachers can enhance their children's learning by providing good hands-on and visual-concept and skill-based experiences such as the following.

Matching:

Can the child find things that are identical in some way such as two identical buttons on a shirt? The ability to discriminate is critical to the development of skills in and beyond math; it also includes prereading skills when there is a need to discriminate between letters such as *b* and *d* or *m* and *w*.

Grouping:

Can the child group items that are not identical but that do have a common relationship? For example, a box of buttons might be regrouped into various colors; ones with two holes or four holes; those that are plastic or wooden; and/or a grouping of those that are identical. When children sort and group objects, they increase observation skills; they look for likenesses, differences, and common relationships. Activities involving grouping and regrouping help with understanding how different things can go together and encourages flexibility and creativity in thinking.

Patterning:

Can the child recognize a repeating sequence of numbers, letters, colors, shapes, sounds? For example, a line of construction paper shapes might be arranged as circle, square, star, circle, square, star, and so forth. Seeing and reproducing patterns helps children see relationships between and among things. The simplest activity of this type is for a child to identify a pattern. The next step is to copy the pattern. Success in these two areas leads to the more difficult activity of creating a pattern for someone else to copy. Patterning can then be extended in a variety of ways: physical movements (hop, hop, jump), clapping games (1 clap, 2 claps, 1 clap) and stories with recurring words or phrases (The House That Jack Built).

Seriation:

Can the child identify what comes next in a series? For example, can he or she arrange different length straws in order from shortest to tallest. This skill extends the concept of grouping by helping children understand that objects that are alike in one way may be different in another. They begin to understand terms such as larger and smaller, shorter and taller, darker and lighter, younger and older.

Beginning Number Concepts:

Can the child recognize, name, reproduce, and understand the concept of numbers? Can he or she find, name, show how many, and write the number 3? This involves a wide variety of skills specifically related to numbers including: (1) *Number identification* by saying a number name; (2) *Rote counting* or saying numbers, such as 1,2,3 in sequential order; (3) *Understanding the quantity* implied by each number, such as show me three fingers; and (4) *One-to-one relationships* such as matching items from one group with items from another to determine if they are equal.

All or Part of:

Can the child understand the relationship between a portion of an object and the entire object? If an apple is cut in half and then in half again, how many pieces are there? Can it be put back together again to make a "whole"? Such sharing experiences eventually lead to an understanding of fraction concepts.

Measuring and Estimating:

Can the child estimate or guess the answer to a problem and then find a way to solve it? For example, how many spoons of rice are needed to fill a particular container? How many popsicle sticks long is the table?

Problem Solving and Reasoning:

Can the child apply math-related thinking skills in everyday situations? How might six cookies be divided between three children? How many more blocks are needed to finish a building project? Such understanding progresses from intuitive to mathematically calculated solutions.

Finally, the authors encourage parents and teachers to use and expand upon the activities provided in *Big Math Activities for Young Children* and to invent others that stimulate each child's interest in mathematical ideas. Try to plan structured experiences and to take advantage of unstructured ones. Attempt to balance the frequency of competitive and cooperative activities. Remember that, when working with young children, there is more to the process than finding a right answer. The act of exploring, discovering, solving problems, and relating to new ideas will allow children to become receptive math learners.